Boeing 777
An American Flagship

Boeing launched the original 777-200 series in October 1990 as an all-new design, though it was originally conceived as a stretched 767. It was the first airliner to be completely developed using a digital base and three-dimensional computer graphics. And at the time of its launch the aircraft featured some other notable firsts. The 777 was Boeing's first use of fly-by-wire control, an advanced glass flight deck featuring five liquid crystal displays and integrated avionics. By empty weight, Boeing used approximately 10% of composites for the aircraft's floor and empennage. Boeing also contracted GE Aviation to design and produce the advanced GE90 high-thrust engine, specifically for the 777.

At its launch, Boeing offered the 777 in two versions, the basic 777-200 and the increased weight, longer range 777-200(IGW) marketed as the 777-200ER (Extra Range). The 777-200 has a range of just over 7,000 nautical miles and the 200ER is graced with 7,725 nautical miles thanks to a new wing centre section fuel tank.

Boeing first flew the 777-200 on June 12, 1994 and gained Federal Aviation Administration certification on April 19, 1995. United Airlines took delivery of the first customer 777-200 aircraft, followed just under two years later by the first 777-200ER to British Airways in February 1997.

Boeing's 777 evolution continued in 1995 with launch of the 300 variant. This stretched version features fuselage plugs fore and aft of the wing amounting to an extra 33ft in length. Further variants followed, the 200LR and the 300ER were launched in February 2002 by Boeing and GE Aircraft Engines at the request of airlines that wanted additional flexibility to serve the nonstop routes demanded by passengers at the time.

Boeing rates the 300ER as the world's most reliable twin-aisle jet and as one of the most successful with over 800 sold.

Boeing did not rest on its 300ER success and opted to launch the new generation 777X family in 2013. The 777-9, the first variant to take flight, is the world's largest twinjet offering promising capabilities and operating economics thanks to the materials, technologies, aerodynamics, its composite wing and the whopping great GE9X engines, each rated at 115,000lb of thrust.

It is a great looking jet, one that will go on to turn heads at airports around the world. Looks are one thing, demand is another. Given the body blow inflicted on the airline industry by the COVID-19 pandemic and the associated slump in passenger demand, once the 777X receives certification Boeing's biggest challenge will be low demand and deferred orders for its new flagship jet. While recovery worldwide from the pandemic continues apace, Boeing has experienced repeated delays with development of the 777X, with deliveries now not expected before the end of 2025 at the earliest – and even that date may be optimistic. When that moment arrives, Boeing says the 777X is well positioned for the future commercial air travel market offering customers the choice to serve a multitude of networks such as long, ultra-long, high and hot, and high-payload missions, or grow an existing market with additional capacity. Watch out for the X!

CONTENTS

6 Classic Triple Sevens
Mark Ayton outlines some major systems of Boeing's classic variants, the 777-200, 777-200ER and the 777-300.

12 Boeing 777-200ER
All the facts and figures.

14 Boeing 777-200LR
The 200LR in numbers.

16 Boeing 777F
Performance, capacities, and tech specs for the freight variant.

18 Three Hundred ER
Editor Mark Ayton outlines the main design features and systems of Boeing's 777-300ER.

20 Boeing 777-300ER
Extended range was the aim of the 300ER.

22 Flight Testing the Boeing 777-300ER
Boeing provides an account of the 777-300ER's 2003 flight test programme.

26 Emirates Lucky 777
Gordon Smith recaps some key moments from the more than 20 years since the 777-300ER launched and chats with a current 777 captain.

30 Improving the Triple Seven
Mark Broadbent details how Boeing enhanced the legacy and second-gen versions of the 777.

36 Triple Seven ecoDemonstrator
In 2018, Boeing's ecoDemonstrator programme used a FedEx 777 Freighter. Mark Broadbent reports.

42 British Airways' Triple Sevens
Boeing's 777 has proved popular with British Airways. Bob O'Brien looks at the Triple Seven's career with BA.

48 Boeing 777 Freighters
Boeing took a gamble on the market being ready for a new-build freighter version of the 777, as detailed by Barry Lloyd.

53 Fully Fledged Freighter
After a near 15 year career flying for Emirates, this Boeing 777-300ER swapped seats and suites for freight.

56 Pima's Boeing 777-200
Mark Ayton covers the donation of the first Boeing 777-200 to the Tucson, Arizona-based Pima Air & Space Museum.

58 Japan's Triple Sevens
The editor reviews the acquisition and operation of two Boeing 777-300ER aircraft by the Japanese Air Self Defense Force.

60 Positively Palatial
Lufthansa Technik's VVIP Boeing BBJ (or Boeing Business Jet) 777-9 concept is aimed squarely at the Middle East, as Ian Harbison discovered.

64 KLM's Triple Seven Transformation
Gordon Smith joined a special flight to Cape Town to meet some of the key players behind the project to overhaul the Dutch flag carrier's widebodies.

70 Boeing's 777X
Mark Broadbent outlines Boeing's new 777X variants, the 777-8 and the 777-9.

76 Boeing's 777-8
Technical specifications for the 777-8.

78 Boeing's 777-9
At an early stage in the evolution of the variant we have the latest characteristics available.

80 Tech File Wing
Mark Broadbent details the design and aerodynamics of the 777X wing.

86 Wing Factory
The 777X's wing is produced in the new Composite Wing Centre at Everett. Mark Broadbent reports on the facility.

92 Tech File Cabin
Mark Broadbent discusses the future cabin experience that will await passengers on board the Boeing 777X.

94 Tech File Engine
Chris Kjelgaard provides a detailed technological description of the GE9X engine powering the Boeing 777X family.

102 777X Milestones
Mark Ayton and Mark Broadbent mark out the 777X's big milestones to date.

108 777X Performance, Production and Flight Testing
With the co-operation of Boeing Commercial Airplanes, Mark Ayton provides the latest details about the 777X programme.

Contents

ISBN: 978 1 80282 999 0
Original editor: Mark Ayton
Updates and amendments this edition: Paul Hamblin
Senior editor, specials: Roger Mortimer
Email: roger.mortimer@keypublishing.com
Cover Design: Steve Donovan
Design: Ros Woodham and SJmagic DESIGN SERVICES, India
Advertising Sales Manager: Sam Clark
Email: sam.clark@keypublishing.com
Tel: 01780 755131
Advertising Production: Becky Antoniades
Email: Rebecca.antoniades@keypublishing.com

SUBSCRIPTION/MAIL ORDER
Key Publishing Ltd, PO Box 300, Stamford, Lincs, PE9 1NA
Tel: 01780 480404
Subscriptions email: subs@keypublishing.com
Mail Order email: orders@keypublishing.com
Website: www.keypublishing.com/shop

PUBLISHING
Group CEO and Publisher: Adrian Cox

Published by
Key Publishing Ltd, PO Box 100, Stamford, Lincs, PE9 1XQ
Tel: 01780 755131 **Website:** www.keypublishing.com

PRINTING
Precision Colour Printing Ltd, Haldane,
Halesfield 1, Telford, Shropshire. TF7 4QQ

DISTRIBUTION
Seymour Distribution Ltd, 2 Poultry Avenue, London, EC1A 9PU
Enquiries Line: 02074 294000.

We are unable to guarantee the bona fides of any of our advertisers. Readers are strongly recommended to take their own precautions before parting with any information or item of value, including, but not limited to money, manuscripts, photographs, or personal information in response to any advertisements within this publication.

© Key Publishing Ltd 2024
All rights reserved. No part of this magazine may be reproduced or transmitted in any form by any means, electronic or mechanical, including photocopying, recording or by any information storage and retrieval system, without prior permission in writing from the copyright owner. Multiple copying of the contents of the magazine without prior written approval is not permitted.

GE AVIATION

BOEING

CLASSICS

ABOVE • AIRTEAMIMAGES/ VICENZO PACE

Since taking its first flight back in 1994, Boeing's largest twin-engine aircraft has evolved through several variants. Prior to the launch of the 777X, the first of five variants was the 777-200, which was followed in chronological order by the 777-200ER (Extended Range), and the stretched 777-300. At the time of its launch, the 777-300 was the longest airliner ever produced measuring 242ft 4in in length. The first three variants are referred to as classics.

Boeing followed up with two further designs, each capable of flying long-range routes, initially the 777-300ER and then the 777-200LR (Long Range). To give some idea of its long-range capability, in 1995 777-200LR N6066Z (c/n 33782), a Boeing test aircraft painted in the company's corporate colours flew eastward from Hong Kong to London completing a non-stop 22-hour and 42-minute flight covering 11,664nm.

The aircraft took off from Hong Kong International Airport with a full load of fuel, and 35 people on board at 22:30pm local time on November 9 and landed at London Heathrow Airport at 13:12pm GMT on November 10. The flight set a world record recognised by the Guinness Book of Records and exceeded the type's baseline design range.

Two of Boeing's pilot crews flew the jet on its epic mission; Captains Darcy-Hennemann and Frank Santoni, and Captains John Cashman and Randy Austin.

Dubbed the Worldliner, the aircraft, a 777-240LR was delivered to Pakistan International Airlines as AP-BGZ on March 23, 2006.

Classic Triple Sevens

Mark Ayton outlines the main design features and systems of Boeing's classic variants, the 777-200, 777-200ER and the 777-300.

777 Tour

All of the 777 classic variants share commonality of the aircraft's main systems. At the time of their respective launches, each variant offered new capability thanks to the design, engineering, materials, and technologies used, details of which are given in this tour of the aircraft's major components and systems.

Fuselage

A legacy 777's fuselage is a pressurized semi-monocoque structure comprising circumferential frames, longitudinal stringers, stressed skin, and pressure bulkheads.

Official documentation shows the 777 fuselage comprises a series of sections. Section 41, the forward section, includes the radome, flight deck, forward pressure bulkhead, nose gear wheel well, main equipment centre, forward cargo door (on the port side), and the forward section of the forward cargo compartment.

Section 43 contains the aft part of the forward cargo compartment.

Sections 44 (upper lobe) and 45 (lower lobe), make up the centre section and contain the wing centre section, the keel beam, and the main gear wheel wells.

Section 46, the section to the aft of 44-45 comprises the aft cargo door (on the port side) and the aft cargo compartment. Section 47 includes the bulk cargo compartment and a bulk cargo door (on the port side).

And section 48 comprises the aft pressure bulkhead, the empennage,

CLASSICS

ABOVE • AIRTEAMIMAGES/ EDWIN CHAI

the stabilizer compartment, the APU compartment, plus its firewall, inlet, and exhaust.

Wing

As with other modern airliners, the 777's wing houses components of the fuel system, attachment points for the engine strut, landing gear, flight control surfaces, and fuel tanks which hold a considerable amount of fuel.

Structurally, the wing comprises front and rear spars, skin panels, stringers, and ribs, all of which are considered the primary structure.

End ribs are sealed to form the ends of the fuel tanks.

Outboard wing sections are connected to the wing centre section by a side-of-body rib, and the main landing gear is attached to the rear wing spar and landing gear beam.

The wing's front spar carries the leading edge slats, and the rear spar carries the trailing edge flaps, ailerons, flaperons and spoilers.

Finally, the 777's wing tip is an aerodynamic fairing fitted to the end of the wing.

Details listed above pertain to the 777-200 and 777-300 versions, the long-range 777-300ER and 777-200LR both feature an extended wing to increase the volume of the fuel tanks with part of the dry wing bay used as part of the centre tank volume.

The 777's elevators, rudder, ailerons, flaperons, flaps, spoilers, strut fairings, engine cowlings and nose gear doors are all made of carbon fibre reinforced plastic (CFRP), primarily to reduce weight but also to counter corrosion. Elevators, rudder, and the tab structure are also made of CFRP, and the panels from fibreglass.

Torque boxes and floor beams are made of toughened CFRP, which is a mix of CFRP and nylon. Toughened CFRP is also used to make torque box spars, ribs, stringers, and skins for the horizontal and vertical stabilisers.

Flight Control Systems

The Boeing 777's primary flight control system (PFCS) is a three-axis, fly-by-wire system. PFCS provides manual and automatic aircraft control and flight envelope protection in all three axes, and stability augmentation in the roll, pitch, and yaw axes. Additionally, the PFCS calculates the commands required to move the control surfaces based on inputs from a variety of sensors.

Two elevators and a moveable horizontal stabilizer provide pitch control, and a tabbed rudder provides yaw control.

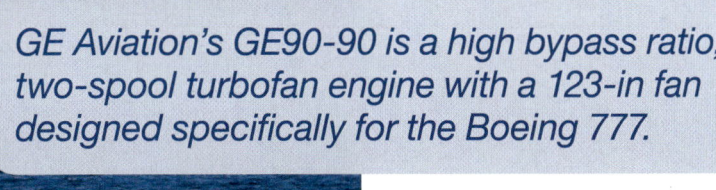

> GE Aviation's GE90-90 is a high bypass ratio, two-spool turbofan engine with a 123-in fan designed specifically for the Boeing 777.

Increased lift required for take-off and landing at lower speeds is provided by a high lift control system comprising a variety of flaps and slats. Each wing is fitted with one double slotted inboard and one single slotted outboard trailing edge flap, and seven leading edge slats and one Krueger flap. The latter element is a lift enhancement device fitted to the leading edge, which seals the gap between the engine strut and the inboard slat.

Leading edge slats operate in one of three positions; retracted (for cruise), sealed (during take-off) and gapped (for landing).

Official documentation says hydraulic or electric motors on the flap power drive unit turn flap torque tubes. The torque tubes operate the flap transmission assemblies, which use a ball screw and gimbal to extend and retract the flaps.

Similarly, hydraulic, or electric motors on the slat power drive unit turn slat torque tubes, which drive rotary actuators, which in turn extend and retract the slats with a rack and pinion drive.

GE90 Engine

GE Aviation's GE90-90 is a high bypass ratio, two-spool turbofan engine designed specifically for the Boeing 777. its main components are a low pressure shaft comprising a 123-inch fan, a three-stage low pressure compressor (or booster), a six-stage low pressure turbine, and a high pressure shaft comprising a ten-stage high pressure compressor and a two-stage high pressure turbine.

Most of the engine's line replaceable units are fitted to the core or the gearbox and accessed by opening the thrust reverser assembly. Others are attached to the fan case accessed by opening the fan cowls.

Two 'big sister' variants, the GE90-110 and GE90-115, power 777-300ER and 777-200LR aircraft.

Main components are a low pressure shaft comprising a 128-inch fan, a four-stage low pressure compressor (or booster) and a six-stage low pressure turbine, a high pressure shaft comprising a nine-stage high pressure compressor and a two-stage high pressure turbine.

All GE90 series engines are equipped with electronic engine controls which use software to set the engine's thrust rating, for example GE90-115 engines have a different take-off thrust rating for the 777-200LR.

Trent 800 Engine

Rolls-Royce's Trent 800 engine is a high bypass ratio, three-spool turbofan with advanced wide-chord fan blades.

Trent engines are fitted with a dual channel full authority digital electronic control (FADEC) system, and an electronic engine controller (EEC) which controls the engine's systems, starts, and auto starts, and thrust reverser operation.

Main components are a low pressure shaft comprising a 110-inch fan, and a five-stage low pressure turbine, an intermediate pressure shaft comprising an eight-stage intermediate pressure compressor, and a single stage intermediate pressure turbine.

A high pressure shaft turns the external gearbox and comprises a six-stage high pressure compressor, and a single stage high pressure turbine.

Rolls-Royce design engineers incorporated a data entry plug accessed externally which selects model-specific software in the EEC to set the engine's thrust rating.

Most line replaceable units are fitted to the engine's fan case or the gearbox (accessed by opening the fan cowl), others are fitted to the engine core accessed by opening the thrust reverser assembly.

Landing Gear

The 777 has a hydraulic pressure operated tricycle landing gear system comprising two main landing gears under the wings and one nose landing gear. Landing gear selector valves control the extension and retraction sequence of operation.

The main landing gears comprise a strut with an air-oil shock absorber, and a drag and a side brace which transfer loads to the aircraft's structure. When the pilot commands the landing gear system to extend, the two wheel well-doors open, and the gear extends. Once the main gear is fully extended down-lock actuators lock the drag brace and side brace in the extended position.

The retraction cycle is a reverse of this process except that up-lock hooks lock the landing gear in the retracted position.

Hydraulic pressure is supplied from the aircraft's triple redundant system. Official documentation says the three hydraulic systems operate independently at 3,000 psi nominal pressure. Named left, centre and right based on the location of their main components, each system has its own reservoir, pumps, and filters.

The left system has an engine-driven pump (EDP) and an alternating current motor pump (ACMP). The right alternating current (AC) bus supplies power to the ACMP. The left system supplies power to the flight controls and the left thrust reverser.

The right system also has an EDP and an ACMP. The left AC bus supplies power to the ACMP. The right system supplies power to the flight controls, the normal main gear brakes, and the right thrust reverser.

CLASSICS

The centre system has two ACMPs, two air-driven pumps (ADPs) and a ram air turbine (RAT) pump. The left and right AC buses supply power to the ACMPs. Pneumatic power from the two engines or the auxiliary power unit (APU) operates the ADPs.

Primary pumps for the left and right systems are the EDPs and the ACMPs in the centre system. These pumps operate continuously.

Demand pumps for the left and right systems are the ACMPs and the ADPs for the centre system. These pumps normally operate only during heavy system demands.

The centre system supplies power to the flight controls, leading edge slats, trailing edge flaps, the alternate and reserve main gear brakes, normal and reserve nose gear steering and nose gear extension-retraction, main gear extension-retraction, and main gear steering.

The RAT deploys automatically during flight when both engines are shut down, when both AC buses are not powered, or when all three hydraulic system pressures are low. Ram air then turns the turbine. Only the flight controls use hydraulic power from the RAT. The RAT can be retracted only on the ground.

Hydraulic pressure enables the doors to open and the main landing gear to extend and retract; all movements are controlled by sequence valves. Hydraulic pressure is automatically removed by the valves once the landing gear is fully retracted.

An alternate extension system enables landing gear extension if the centre hydraulic system has no pressure. The alternate extend power pack supplies hydraulic pressure to release the landing gear doors and the landing gear. The doors open, and the gear extends by their own weight. The gear doors stay open after an alternate extension.

Each main landing gear truck has three axles and six wheels, interestingly the aft axle pivots to steer the main gear, minimise the turn radius and prevent tyre scrub.

When extended in flight, the main landing gear trucks tilt approximately 13° forward in a wheels up attitude. Conversely, when the gear is retracted and locked the trucks tilt approximately 5° forward in a wheels down attitude.

The nose landing gear comprises a strut with an air-oil shock absorber, and a drag brace (one that folds) which transfers load to the aircraft's structure. The drag brace is locked in position by a hydraulically powered lock link when the nose gear is either fully extended or retracted.

The nose gear wheel well has two sets of doors, forward and aft. Forward doors operate hydraulically during gear retraction and extension while the aft doors are mechanically operated by linkages connected to the nose gear. Consequently, the aft doors only close when the gear retracts.

Just like the main landing gears, extension and retraction of the nose landing gear is powered by a centre hydraulic pressure system, with all movement of both the forward door and landing gear controlled by sequence valves.

Nose gear alternate extension uses hydraulic pressure from the alternate extend power pack. The forward doors open, and the landing gear extends by its own weight. The forward doors stay open after an alternate extension.

Two tillers (small steering wheels) control nose wheel movement to a maximum of 70° in each direction and the rudder pedals control nose wheel movement to a maximum of 7° in each direction.

When a nose wheel steering command exceeds 13°, the main gear steering control unit receives tiller position data and controls the aft axles to steer up to 8° left or right, once again powered by hydraulic pressure.

Whenever steering commands are not being input to the system, actuators align all forward and aft wheels and lock the steerable aft axles.

Each main gear wheel has a carbon brake (there are no brakes on the nose landing gear), controlled by an autobrake function within the brake system control unit which limits antiskid. The 777's brake system has temperature monitoring and tyre pressure indication functions.

Brakes are controlled from two sets of pedals connected by cables to the left and right brake metering valves. The valves provide hydraulic pressure to the brakes in proportion to the pedal movement. In the event that

> The 777's flight deck is equipped with six large flat panel high resolution, full colour, active matrix, liquid crystal display units; the two outboards show primary flight displays, the left and right inboards tend to be used as navigational displays showing navigational information.

hydraulic pressure is not available for both normal and back-up braking, the crew receive alerts. In this situation, a brake accumulator supplies sufficient pressure for five full brake applications.

Flight Deck

The 777's flight deck is equipped with six 8" x 8" flat panel high resolution, full colour, active matrix, liquid crystal display units (DUs); the two outboards show primary flight displays (PFDs),

ABOVE • AIRTEAMIMAGES/ DEREK MACPHERSON

the left and right inboards tend to be used as navigational displays showing navigational information or in multi-function formats.

Upper centre shows the engine indicating and crew alerting system, and the lower centre tends to be used to display multi-function formats. Displays with multi-function formats are controlled using either of the two cursor control devices located on the control stand. These touch-sensitive pads enable the flight crew to control the cursor on the active display.

Each PFD uses a single format, showing the aircraft's attitude, airspeed, barometric altitude, vertical speed, heading, flight modes, radio altitude, ILS data, TCAS advisories and time critical warnings. Navigational displays show VOR, APP (approach), map and plan display modes. Multi-function displays show auxiliary information such as secondary engine, communication, or a checklist.

Flight Management Computing System

The 777's flight management computing system (FMCS) is designed to decrease flight crew work load by giving vertical and lateral guidance for all phases of flight except take-off and landing.

All three inner DUs are used to interface with the FMCS which is used to display navigation, flight planning, performance management information, and auto tunes the navigation radios for position and display updates.

Boeing 777-200ER

Boeing 777-200ER Characteristics

Wingspan	199ft 11in
Length	209ft 1in
Height	60ft 9in
Max take-off weight	656,000lb
Max landing weight	460,000lb
Max zero fuel weight	430,000lb
Operating empty weight	304,500lb
Max structural payload	125,550lb
Total cargo volume	5,330ft^3
Useable fuel	45,220 US gal
Cruise speed	Mach 0.84
Ceiling	41,000ft
Seating	Up to 313 passengers two-class
Range	7,065 nautical miles
Engines	Two GE90-94Bs, PW4000s or Rolls-Royce Trent 870s-Trent 895s

Data: Boeing

AIR TEAMIMAGES/ALVIN MAN

Boeing 777-200LR

Boeing 777-200LR Characteristics

Wingspan	212ft 7in
Length	209ft 1in
Height	61ft 1in
Max take-off weight	766,000lb
Max landing weight	492,000lb
Max zero fuel weight	461,000lb
Operating empty weight	320,000lb
Max structural payload	141,000lb
Total cargo volume	5,330ft^3
Useable fuel	47,890 US gal
Cruise speed	Mach 0.84
Ceiling	41,000ft
Seating	Up to 317 passengers two-class
Range	8,555 nautical miles
Engines	Two GE90-110B1s/ GE90-115B1s

Data: Boeing

Boeing 777F

Boeing 777F Characteristics

Wingspan	212ft 7in
Length	209ft 1in
Height	61ft 1in
Max take-off weight	766,800lb
Max landing weight	575,000lb
Max zero fuel weight	547,000lb
Operating empty weight	318,300lb
Max structural payload	228,700lb
Total cargo volume	23,051ft³
Useable fuel	47,890lb
Cruise speed	Mach 0.84
Ceiling	41,000ft
Range	4,970 nautical miles
Engines	Two GE90-110B1s/ GE90-115B1s

Data: Boeing

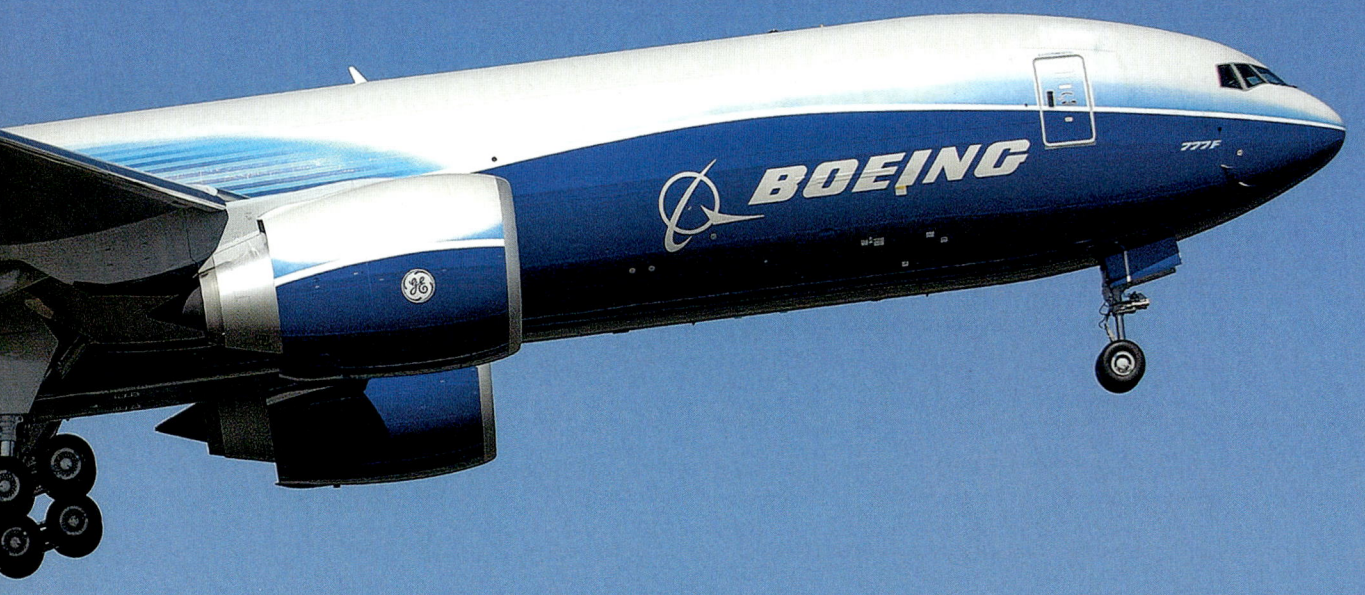

BOEING

BOEING 777-300ER

Three Hundred

AIRTEAMIMAGES/
ALVIN MAN

Boeing's 777-300ER is a more extensive development of the original variants, with increased MCTOW and fuel capacity to extend range up to 7,930 nautical miles. Boeing designed the 300ER to serve the point-to-point market. Major changes include strengthened structure for the higher operating weights; extended wing box and new raked wingtip extension; new nose and semi-levered main landing gear; a tail-strike protection system; revised struts and nacelles; and uprated GE90 engines rated at 115,000lb.

At the time of its launch, the 777-300ER usurped the 777-300 becoming the largest and most powerful twin-engine aircraft ever developed. The 300ER is another example of Boeing's payload and range evolution for its 777 widebody jet.

To make the 300ER reality, Boeing was entirely dependent on the development of an engine type powerful enough to lift the monster aloft. Boeing did not have to search too far or too wide to find the right motor. GE Aviation which developed the GE90 specifically for the original 777, developed the GE90-115B turbofan featuring large composite blades, with a fan diameter of 128in.

In the spring of 2003, GE Aviation completed a highly successful flight test programme with the GE90-115B engine on the company's 747 testbed aircraft, a unique flying test laboratory designed to accumulate comprehensive in-flight data on new GE engine models before they are installed on a customer aircraft.

According to GE Aviation, configured with a GE90-115B engine installed on the left inboard position, the 747 completed 48 flights and 217 flight hours over a 152-day period. Data at altitude conditions was obtained, essential for the engine's development and certification and not available from a ground test programme.

Comprehensive in nature, the flight test programme focussed on performance, air start capability, and system durability. Chaker Chahrour, general manager of the GE90 engine programme said: "The first flight set the

ER

Mark Ayton outlines the main design features and systems of Boeing's 777-300ER.

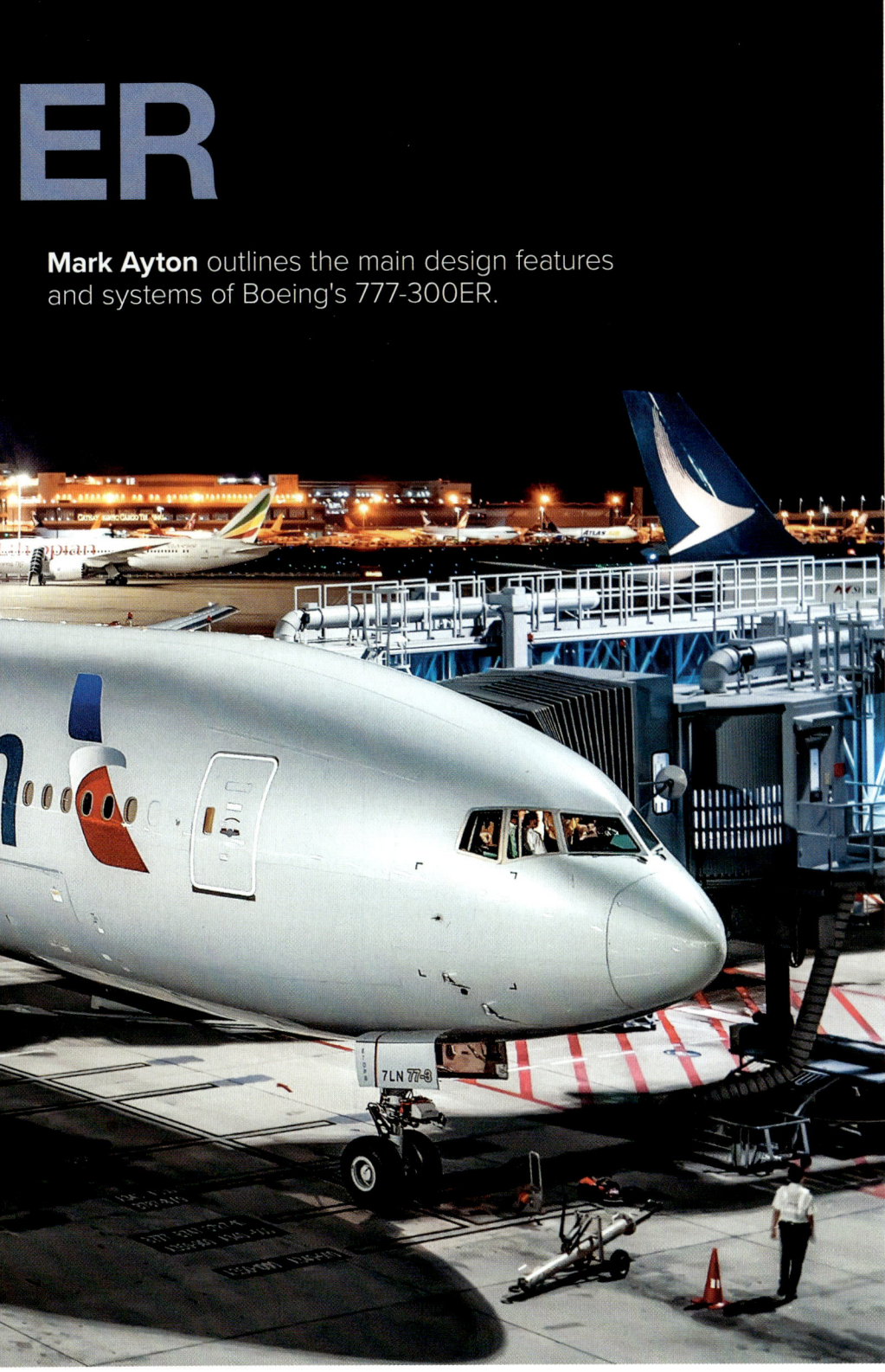

tone for the programme. Subsequent testing was aggressive and verified the altitude performance and durability of the GE90-115B design."

Al Krejmas, manager of engineering programmes at GE's Flight Test Operation in California said: "We obtained valuable data to support Boeing's engine/aircraft FAR25 certification programme before the first flight of the Boeing 777-300ER."

Following the 777-300ER's first flight in February 2003, Boeing's flight test department entered a 12-month flight-test programme using three aircraft.

The 777-300ER's flight deck retains the same layout as the 777-200 and 777-300 variants comprising six larger high-resolution, full colour, active matrix, liquid crystal display units (DUs). Two outboards show primary flight displays (PFDs), the left and right inboards tend to be used as navigational displays, the upper centre shows the engine indicating and crew alerting system, and the lower centre tends to be used to display multi-function formats. Like classic 777 flight decks, pilots use touch pad cursor control devices to move display cursors.

For an aircraft with the length of the 777-300ER, preventing a tail strike is critical, such an event is more likely if the pilot commands the aircraft to rotate too soon or too fast. Boeing has developed a solution for this by including a tail strike protection system in the pitch axis flight control laws.

A mix of the aircraft's aerodynamic, weight and loading parameters determine the optimal nose-up pitch angle of the jet on take-off. For an aircraft as long as the 777-300ER the nose-up pitch angle has limits to minimise the risk of a tail strike. On take-off, as the aircraft climbs away from the runway, nose-up rotation relative to the ground and rate of climb affect the movement of the tail. The slower the take-off speed, the greater the nose-up rotation, the closer the aircraft's tail to the runway.

Boeing embedded its tail protection system in the aircraft's fly-by-wire flight control system which enables continuous monitoring of the aircraft's performance data, computation of the aircraft's tail location relative to the runway and the tail's rate of closure to the ground during take-off.

Should the system sense an imminent tail strike an automatic command is sent to the flight control system to rotate the elevators to invoke a nose-down attitude up to 10° to avoid a strike.

The system also optimises the aircraft's aerodynamic performance on take-off and landing, enabling greater payloads.

Externally, a 777-300ER is almost identical to a 300, except for the 6ft 6in-long raked wingtip extensions and the colossal GE90-115 series engines. To meet load bearing requirements for carrying higher gross weights, the aircraft's structure is strengthened, and the main landing gear has a semi-levered arrangement which shifts rotation from the main axle (centre) to the aft axle. The semi-levered arrangement comprises a hydraulic diagonal strut connecting the forward part of the truck to the top of the main strut. When the aircraft rotates, the hydraulic diagonal strut locks keeping the truck perpendicular to the main strut. This causes the aircraft to rotate about the aft axle which increases the height of the main gear by around 12in.

777-300ER

Boeing 777-300ER Characteristics

Wingspan	212ft 7in
Length	242ft 4in
Height	60ft 8in
Max take-off weight	775,000lb
Max landing weight	554,000lb
Max zero fuel weight	524,000lb
Operating empty weight	370,000lb
Max structural payload	154,000lb
Total cargo volume	7,120ft^3
Useable fuel	47,890 US gal
Cruise speed	Mach 0.84
Ceiling	41,000ft
Seating	Up to 396 passengers two-class
Range	7,370 nautical miles
Engines	Two GE90-115B1s

Data: Boeing

Boeing 777-300ER

AIRTEAM IMAGES/
MARKUS MAINKA

FLIGHT TESTING

Flight-testing the
777-300ER

Boeing Frontiers' **Debbie Heathers** provides an account of the flight testing programme that went into the Boeing 777-300ER.

Flight testing of the Boeing 777-300ER began on February 24, 2003 with the first flight of WD501, the first flight-test aircraft. A second flight-test aircraft, WD502, entered the flight-test programme in early April of that year.

Frank Santoni, 777 chief test pilot said: "We typically go to Iceland for the crosswinds and tailwinds, to South America for the natural ice, and to the Australian outback for hot weather. We go to airports outside of our home base of Puget Sound to test, because they are more efficient for the different types of testing required."

The team performed its critical tests at Edwards because it's not too busy with other traffic and has long runways.

While at remote assignments engineers tested the aircraft under extreme conditions, from -29°F and foggy in Glasgow, Montana, to -54°F in Canada's Baffin Islands, to 95°F and humid in Singapore to dry and 112°F in Alice Springs, Australia.

While at the locations every replaceable component must be tested, removed, and replaced in a variety of harsh environments.

Launching a new aircraft's flight-testing process involves a huge investment of time. According to Larry Muri, lead flight-test mechanic, the flight-test team is responsible for verifying compatibility, durability, longevity and maintainability of each aircraft, the associated components, and any innovations.

Work of preparing for a flight test begins before the aircraft is built. Schedules and tests are approved before the aircraft gets to the production stage. Once the aircraft is airborne and lands safely after completing its first flight, comprehensive tests begin and continue nearly around the clock for months.

Changes Are Primary Focus

In order to certify the 777-300ER to enter passenger service, the FAA required Boeing to perform numerous tests. Many of the tests for the 777-300ER were a result of changes from earlier 777 models: the 777-200, 777-200ER and 777-300.

The 777-300ER extended the 777-300's range by more than 1,700 nautical miles to 7,420 nautical miles or is able to carry an additional 55,000lb of cargo.

Other changes to the 777-300ER included.
- Extending each wing by 6ft 6in and adding raked wingtips to improve the overall aerodynamic efficiency.

RIGHT • *One of Boeing's 777-300ER flight test aircraft, registration N5017V, during a test flight.* BOEING

LEFT • *Boeing mechanics position a mobile jack to be used to change the wheels on a 777-300ER after maximum brake testing.* BOEING

While operating out of Edwards, the WD501 team conducted numerous Boeing and FAA certification tests including take-off performance, abuse take-offs and ground minimum control speed tests.

FLIGHT TESTING

Raked wingtips, similar to those on the 767-400ER, help reduce take-off field length, increase climb performance, and reduce fuel burn.

- Strengthening the aircraft's body, wing, empennage, and nose gear to support the increased take-off weight of 775,000lb.

- Installing new main landing gear, wheels, tyres, and brakes.

- Adding a supplementary electronic tailskid. This software feature helps prevent inadvertent scraping of the tail on the runway at take-off or landing by commanding elevator movement if the aircraft's nose-up attitude exceeds pre-set limits.

- Modifying the struts and nacelles to accommodate the significantly higher-thrust engines.

- Providing a new higher-thrust derivative of the General Electric GE90 engine.

The Pilot's Role

Boeing Commercial Airplanes pilot Frank Santoni was involved in the 777 since the testing of the first aircraft in the programme.

"Not even 20% of what we do is flying the aircraft," Santoni said. "In addition to being pilots, we're also engineers. We work with engineering and manufacturing to build new features."

"It's a great job if you like to fly, but it's a different job from that of an airline pilot," Santoni said. "We not only test the aircraft in the typical flight envelope, but we also spend a great deal of time outside of where an airline pilot will fly. This ensures the aircraft behaves as expected should it ever be exposed to these unusual conditions. We also are faced with understanding and evaluating any changes we introduce due to discoveries during our testing."

The idea of a test programme is not to take an aircraft beyond its limits; the purpose is to find the limits so warning systems can be set to prevent pilots from reaching those limits.

"We help make changes that improve the aircraft's performance, passenger comfort and the pilot's ability to fly the aircraft," Santoni said.

Boeing's policy for flight-testing allows only pilots to be on board for an airplane's first flight. Gradually, essential personnel, such as engineers and flight-test crew are allowed on board to perform analysis.

"These folks can make decisions and change testing immediately, if needed," Santoni said. "We beam the data to the ground, but we also can analyse the data while we're still in the air. The on board crew is able to perform three or four experiments to maximize our time and minimize costs."

Not Your Typical Aircraft

The 242-foot-long 777-300ER test aircraft was filled with rows of computer workstations and printers, racks of data storage and 45 sixty-gallon water barrels. During flights, an engineer moved water among the barrels, shifting the weight between

RIGHT • *Some of the 45 sixty-gallon water barrels on board a 777-300ER flight test aircraft. For test purposes, engineers moved water among the barrels to shift the weight between the front and rear of the aircraft to alter the aircraft's centre of gravity.* BOEING

BELOW • *A Boeing flight test crew shelter from torrential rain underneath a 777-300ER aircraft during brake testing.* BOEING

While at remote assignments engineers tested the aircraft under extreme conditions, from -29°F and foggy in Glasgow, Montana, to -54°F in Canada's Baffin Islands, to 95°F and humid in Singapore to dry and 112°F in Alice Springs, Australia.

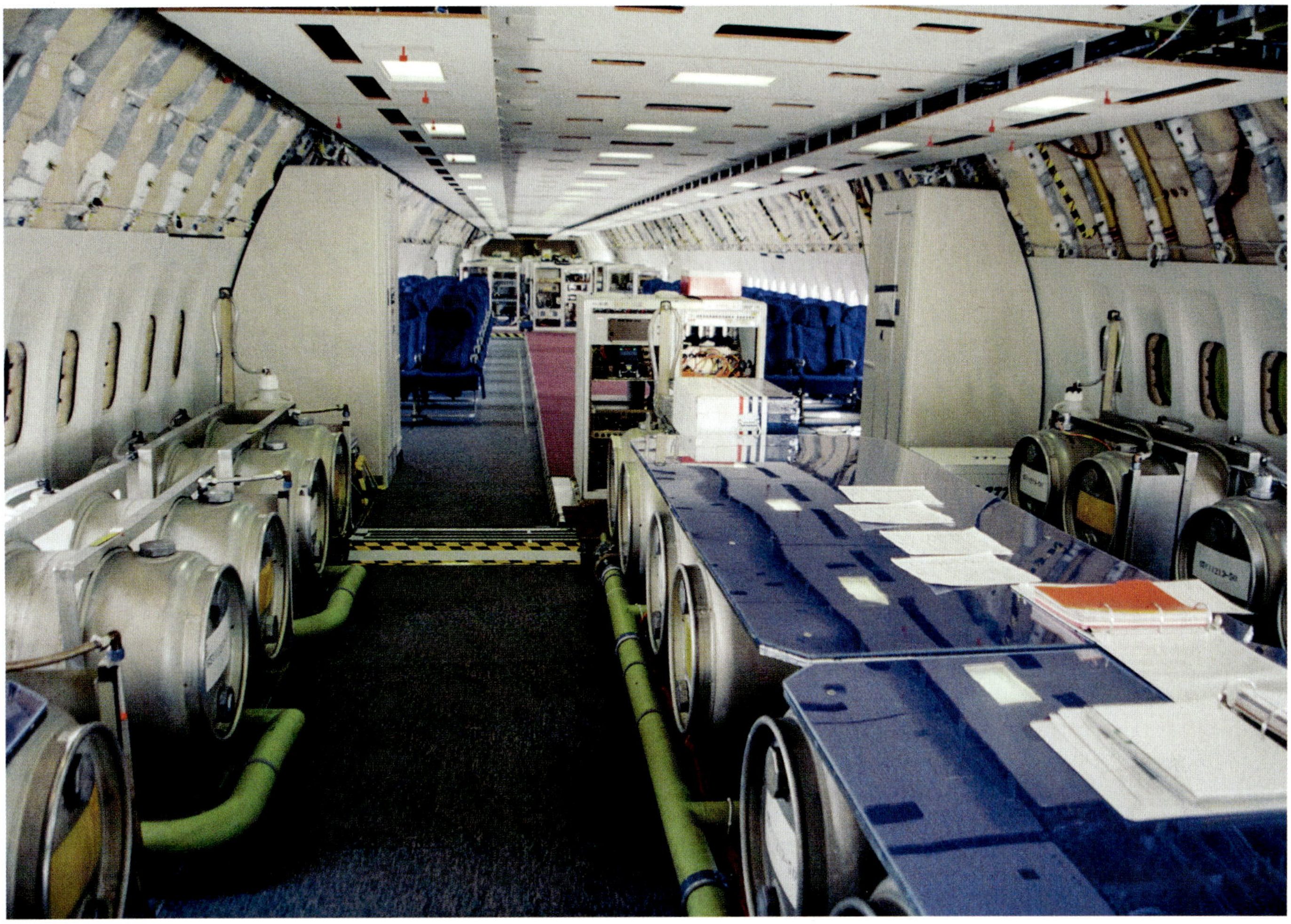

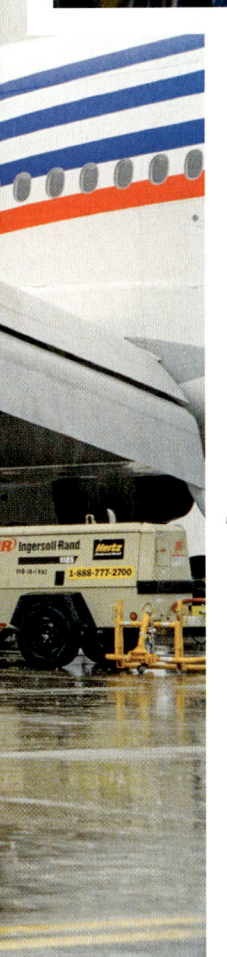

the front and rear of the aircraft, to change the aircraft's centre of gravity.

Computer workstations allow engineers to view what's happening on the flight deck. Video screens show the pilot's flight and navigation displays, and each screen includes a digital time stamp. If something goes wrong, the videotape relays can pinpoint the exact sequence of events.

At the rear of the aircraft is a giant reel that houses a trailing cone. The cone is dragged behind the aircraft during flight and measures the static pressure (altitude) behind the aircraft. During the test, the cone is extended up to 125ft behind the aircraft, so the instrument is outside the pressure field created by the aircraft as it moves through the air.

Hundreds of Tests

In the early stages of the flight-test programme, initial testing focussed on clearing all major facets of the basic flight envelope required prior to the granting of Type Inspection Authority (TIA) by the FAA. Once the team obtained TIA in mid-March 2003, it began testing immediately, interspersing certification tests along with ongoing engineering tests.

Types of certification tests scheduled included maximum gross weight take-offs, check climbs, stall-speed performance, and buffet-boundary performance. Engineering data collection involves brake anti-skids tuning, brake system control unit software evaluations, tail strike protection development, landing gear actuation evaluation, as well as a number of other tests.

While operating out of Edwards, the WD501 team conducted numerous Boeing and FAA certification tests including take-off performance, abuse take-offs and ground minimum control speed tests.

Other tests at Edwards included stability and control, air minimum control speed, stall characteristics, GE90-115B engine 15-knot tail wind and inlet compatibility demonstrations, and flight control modal suppression function evaluations.

To maximize the time at Edwards, mornings were reserved for runway work. Edwards has a 15,000ft long runway, which allows pilots to evaluate the aircraft's take-off performance. In the afternoons, when the winds pick up, stability and control flights were scheduled.

During the late summer, continuing through the third quarter, both aircraft were used for extended operations and systems trials.

The FAA and EASA certifications granted an amended type certificate for the 777, as well as a production certificate, which authorized Boeing to build the 777-300ER.

International Lease Finance Corporation's customer Air France received the first 777-300ER in April 2004.

The testing at Edwards was just one part of the 777-300ER's 1,600-hour flight- and 1,000-hour ground-test programme, which culminated in certification of the aircraft by the FAA in March 2004. Three 777-300ER flight test aircraft were involved.

According to Boeing, the thorough and rigorous test programme demonstrated the aircraft's capabilities, often in extreme environments such as frigid Yakutsk, Russia and sweltering Alice Springs, Australia. Major test activities included aerodynamics, stability and control, flight controls, structures, and systems.

Excellent performance during flight testing led Boeing to offer the airplane with higher range and payload capabilities than planned; the 777-300ER carries 365 passengers up to 7,705 nautical miles.

The 777 Lucky Number Seven

Believe it or not, it's over 20 years since the first flight of the Boeing 777-300ER. To mark the milestone, **Gordon Smith** recaps some of the pioneering achievements of this best-selling aircraft, before speaking to a current 777 captain.

The Boeing 777-300ER made its first flight on February 24, 2003 with its maiden delivery to Air France following on April 29, 2004. Not only is the -300ER the largest member of Boeing's commercial aircraft portfolio to be delivered (ahead of the upcoming 777X), the 'ER' or extended range model is also the best-selling variant of any member of the 777 Family.

To trace the origins of this incredible jet, we need to look back to June 1995 when Boeing's original 777 offering entered service. It proved popular, but to offer airlines additional flexibility in serving non-stop routes, the US manufacturer later introduced a pair of even longer range products. Alongside the delivery of the first 777-300ER in 2004 – which can carry 365 passengers up to 7,930nm (14,685km) – in February 2006 the maiden 777-200LR 'Worldliner' (Longer Range) entered service, with a range of up to 9,290nm (17,205 km) when carrying 314 passengers.

Widebody Pioneer

While it is no longer the most technologically advanced aircraft on the market, when it first arrived on the scene, the 777 was transformational. Highlights included an innovative wing design, with a span of 199ft 11in (60.9m) to enhance its ability to achieve higher speeds, climb quickly and cruise at higher altitudes than competing models.

The wings also allow the aircraft to carry full passenger payloads out of many high-elevation, high-temperature (so-called 'hot and high') airfields. The 777-200LR and 777-300ER sport 6.5ft (1.9m) wingtips to improve the overall aerodynamic efficiency which help reduce take-off field length, increase

Aircraft Statistics

	777-200LR	777-300ER
Seats (typical two-class configuration)	317	396
Range	8,555nm (15,843km)	7,370nm (13,649km)
Length	209ft 1in (63.7m)	242ft 4in (73.9m)
Wingspan	212ft 7in (64.8m)	212ft 7in (64.8 m)
Height	61ft 1in (18.6m)	60ft 8in (18.5 m)
Engine	GE90-115BL	GE90-115BL

Source: Boeing

BELOW • *Emirates' Boeing 777-300ER, A6-EQP (c/n 42363) pictured on the apron at its Dubai home. The example was the final -300ER to be delivered new to the carrier.* EMIRATES

RIGHT • *Emirates accepted its 100th 777-300ER in 2014.* BOEING

RIGHT • *Emirates' final 777 Delivery: 777-300ER A6-EQP on November 30, 2018.* EMIRATES

climb performance, and reduce fuel burn.

One of the other reasons the 777-300ER has been so popular is its twin-engine design. Although it is commonplace today, 20 years ago the market for quadjets was still buoyant with the A340 and 747 flying high and the A380 yet to arrive on the scene.

In total, three engine manufacturers developed turbofans to power the mighty 777. General Electric with its GE90 series, Rolls-Royce's Trent 800 series and Pratt & Whitney's PW4000s. However, for the longer range 777 models and the 777 Freighter, GE is the exclusive engine supplier with its GE90-115B and GE90-110B.

In contrast to earlier generation models, the powerplants boast larger-diameter fans with wide-chord fan blade designs and bypass ratios ranging from six-to-one to as high as nine-to-one. This compares to a more typical five-to-one ratio seen on older twin-engine aircraft.

Futuristic Design

While it has since been leapfrogged by the latest composite technologies, such as those found on the 787 Dreamliner, the 777 was well ahead of its time with the use of lightweight, cost-effective structural materials that lessen the overall weight of the aircraft and contribute to fuel efficiency.

Among the most notable features is an aluminium alloy in the upper wing skin and stringers. Known as '7055', it offers greater compression strength than previous concepts which enabled designers to save weight and improve corrosion and fatigue resistance. Elsewhere, carbon fibres embedded in toughened resins are found in the 777's vertical and horizontal tails. The floor beams of the passenger cabin are also made of these special materials. According to Boeing, composites, including resins and adhesives, account for approximately nine percent of the 777's structural weight. This compares with around 50% for the 787 Dreamliner.

A feature unique at the time to the 777-300ER and 777-300 flight deck is the Ground Manoeuvre Camera System (GMCS). This is designed

Boeing 777 total deliveries by type

777-200	88
777-200ER	422
777-200LR	61
777-300	60
777-300ER	832
777F	238
777X (pending)	Has 374 orders as of spring, 2024
Total	1,722

Source: Boeing

LUCKY 777

FAR LEFT • *The -300ER is the largest Boeing commercial aircraft currently in revenue service.* AIRTEAMIMAGES.COM/4X6ZK MONI SHAFIR

LEFT • *Captain Krisztián Bártfai flies the Boeing 777 around the world, with short regional hops and ultra long-haul trips part of his regular schedule.* EMIRATES

to assist the pilots in the safe movement of the aircraft while on the ground with camera views of the nose gear and main gear areas. The cameras are located on the leading edge of the left and right horizontal stabilisers and the underside of the fuselage. These valuable images are displayed at the multi-functional display positions in the flight deck in a three-way split format.

Looking below the primary fuselage, the main landing gear for the 777 is in a standard two-post arrangement, however it features six-wheel trucks, instead of more traditional four-wheel units. This provides a total of 12 wheels for better weight distribution on runways and taxi areas, and avoids the need for a supplemental two-wheel gear under the centre of the fuselage. Upon its entry to service, the 777's landing gear was the largest ever incorporated into a commercial aircraft and due to its even longer length, the 777-300ER applies a semi-levered gear, which allows it to take off from airports with shorter runways.

Since its first flight over 20 years ago, Boeing has sought to improve the 777-300ER by adopting advances in technology. The US firm says numerous software upgrades and other enhancements have led to an increase in range of 630nm (1,166km) and airframe maintenance cost decreases of 13%. As the platform has matured, additional efficiencies have been identified. The latest maintenance programme for the 777-300ER has increased the intervals between many tasks. Boeing suggests this saves more than 400 labour hours per aircraft per year – the equivalent of an extra day of revenue service annually for every 777 in the fleet.

From The Flight Deck

Emirates is the world's biggest operator of the Boeing 777-300ER. In December 2018, the Dubai-based carrier celebrated a fleet milestone with the delivery of the final Boeing 777-300ER aircraft on its order books. Registered A6-EQP (c/n 42363), it was the 190th 777 example to be delivered to the carrier, and the 146th delivery of a -300ER variant. which is the only airline in the world to have operated all the six variants of the 777 Family.

To celebrate the anniversary of the Boeing 777-300ER, and to learn more about the jet, we caught up with Captain Krisztián Bártfai, a member of Emirates 777 flight deck crew. With one of out every eight 777s manufactured by Boeing delivered to Emirates, there's no one better to speak to in order to learn more about this remarkable aircraft.

ALW: How do Emirates Boeing 777s compare to other fleets?
CKB: One of the benefits of being an Emirates pilot is that you get to work with one of the youngest airline fleets in the world – including more than 140 Boeing 777s. We have two configurations – the 777-300ER and the 777-200LR. There are a few differences in terms of the engines we fly, as well as their maximum range. The 777-300ER's engine has slightly more thrust than the 777-200LR (115,540lbs versus 110,760lbs) but has a reduced maximum range (7,880nm versus 9,420nm).

ALW: The 777 is a real workhorse for Emirates. Can you provide some insight into how the fleet is utilised?
CKB: Our fleet of Boeing 777s flies to nearly 130 cities across six continents, carrying millions of passengers across the globe each year. The 777-300ER, for example, can also carry around 18 tonnes of cargo and Emirates SkyCargo uses the fleet to transport a range of products – from fresh produce to pharma, even cars. We also have a fleet of dedicated Boeing freighters for transporting goods, and we've also recently announced a new order for five new 777-200LR freighter aircraft.

ALW: Emirates operates the 777 on shorter routes as well as long-haul flights – what would a normal day look like when operating a regional service?
CKB: Our duty day regularly involves a two-sector trip – and so we do return back to Dubai. There are many destinations in the region with a short duration of a couple of hours, such as Oman or Bahrain. As we are a full service airline, the preparation time between flights is relatively longer when it comes to a turnaround service.

LEFT • *Emirates operates an all-widebody fleet comprising the 777 and Airbus A380.* AIRTEAMIMAGES.COM/ ROHAN PATEL

Emirates and the Boeing 777 family

Jun 1996	Emirates receives delivery of its first Boeing 777 aircraft A6-EMD (c/n 27247) a -200 variant
Jun 2003	Emirates announces order for 26 777-300ERs at the 2003 Paris Air Show, worth US$5.6bn at list prices
Mar 2005	Emirates receives its first 777-300ER
2009	Emirates becomes the world's largest operator of the 777
Nov 2013	Emirates makes aviation history with a record-breaking order for 150 777X
Oct 2014	Emirates receives its 100th 777-300ER
Sep 2015	Emirates receives its 150th 777
Nov 2016	Emirates starts taking delivery of its new generation -300ER with enhanced business class seats and improved performance
Nov 2017	Emirates unveils new cabins for its 777 fleet including fully enclosed private suites in first class
2023	Emirates intends to return all of its fleet to service after the COVID-19 crisis
2025?	Emirates due to receive first 777X

Source: Emirates

ALW: What is the Emirates' process in graduating pilots onto flying 777s?
CKB: The widebody Boeing 777 is such a large and complex aircraft that it requires pilots to fulfil quite a few criteria before they can fly it. If you are successful, there are more assessments and training to go through before you get the chance to be added to the flying roster. Emirates' pilots complete robust training programmes with highly skilled instructors in Emirates' training facility, which houses full-flight simulators for Boeing 777s.

ALW: Can you describe a typical day 'in the office'?
CKB: I start my mornings with some brief exercise and get ready to start the day. As pilots we enjoy free accommodation and free transport to and from work, which is a great perk. I check in at Emirates Group Headquarters and have a briefing with our flight deck colleagues and cabin crew. We then board the flight – and after 26 years of flying, I am still amazed how grand and beautiful the Boeing 777 aircraft is. The pre-flight phase is generally very busy and our journey kicks off once the aircraft is pushed back.

ALW: What about operational elements of the 777 once in the air?
CKB: During cruising altitude, we keep a close eye on actual fuel burn as compared to what was planned, monitoring route alternates for weather, etc. The view from the cockpit is second to none. For example, the far North Atlantic routes mostly take us over the Greenland and Canadian wilderness which is an incredible sight.

During descent preparation we might be planning for two or more possible runways of varying length meaning different braking considerations, different types of instrument approaches, what route to take, where the aircraft is parked upon landing, etc. Once parked and all customers have disembarked there is still plenty of work to be done, especially for our cabin crew. Once we clear airport formalities, we head to our hotel, freshen up and discover the city.

ALW: What are your favourite destinations when flying the 777?
CKB: I enjoy trips with a longer layover – such as the USA or Australia – and of course, my home Budapest. I like to exercise as much as I can during layovers – whether it's running, biking or hiking. It's always great to discover new destinations and cultures. I would like to think I've left my GPS footprint everywhere across the world – close to a Guinness record! Having said that, some months I also like to stay in Dubai so I bid for 'turnarounds' and I use that time to coach my sons kayaking or ice hockey (yes we play ice hockey in the UAE!).

BELOW • *An Emirates 777-300ER departing Seattle for a return to the Middle East.* AIRTEAMIMAGES.COM/ JOHN KILMER

ALW: What are the longest and shortest Emirates 777 scheduled flights?
CKB: The shortest Boeing 777 flight is between Dubai and Muscat at 187nm (349km). The longest is from Dubai to Dallas-Fort Worth at 6,987nm (12,940km).

 DON'T MISS OUT ON OTHER KEY AVIATION MAGAZINE SPECIALS
If you'd like to be kept informed about Key Publishing's aviation books, magazine specials, subscription offers and the latest product releases. **Scan here »**

Improving the Triple Seven

Mark Broadbent details how Boeing enhanced the legacy and second-gen versions of the 777.

More than 800 777-300ERs have now been ordered. This one, Saudi Arabian Airlines 777-3FG/ER HZ-AK40 (c/n 61598), is pictured taxiing at Paris CDG in April 2017.
AIRTEAMIMAGES/ MATTHEW DOUHAIRE

IMPROVING

Six Triple Seven variants have entered service to date: the 777-200, the 777-200ER, the 777-300, the 777-300ER, the ultra-long-range 777-200LR and the 777 Freighter.

The 777-300ER is the stand-out performer from a sales perspective. By March 2024 it accounted for 832 of all legacy and second-gen Triple Sevens ordered. Boeing has sold 422 777-200ERs, 61 777-200LRs and 264 777Fs. Of the out-of-production models, the company sold 88 777-200s and 60 777-300s.

Key reasons for the 777-300ER's particular success include its 7,370 nautical mile range, high capacity (392 seats in a standard two-class configuration), twin-engine economics and 7,120ft3 of lower deck cargo capacity, which gives operators valuable incremental revenue-earning opportunities.

Triple Sevens have been delivered to more than 60 operators worldwide. Dubai-based Emirates has more in service than any other airline.

Performance Improvement Package

With a popular product on its hands and such a large established customer base, it isn't surprising Boeing has sought to improve the 777.

In 2009, the company realised some technologies developed for the 777-300ER could be retro fitted to the earlier models and introduced a Performance

The 2015 Performance Improvement Package is available not just as the standard configuration for the 777-300ER and 777F, but also as retrofits for in-service aircraft.

ABOVE • *The 2015 Performance Improvement Package includes a divergent trailing edge, which increases the camber (or the asymmetry between a wing's top and bottom surfaces), which in turn increases airflow over the wing.* AIRTEAMIMAGES/ MEHRAD WATSON

TOP LEFT • *Qatar Airways was the launch customer for the 2015 Performance Improvement Package, which will be applied to all its 777-300ERs.* BOEING

LEFT • *Around 0.5% of the 2% fuel burn reduction introduced by the 2015 improvement package comes from a Fuel Burn Upgrade for the GE90 turbofan engines. Boeing also introduced lighter wheels and brakes for the aircraft.* AIRTEAMIMAGES/ RUDI BOIGELOT

Improvement Package (PIP) for the 777-200, 777-200ER and 777-300.

The 2009 PIP introduced three key changes. The first was an upgraded ram-air turbine system to provide improved control of airflow and thrust recovery. The second change was a drooped aileron, a software-based modification was designed to create a higher aerodynamic loading on the outboard wing to make the loading more elliptical and cut drag. The third change was the replacement of 32 vortex generators by smaller 737-type vortex generators to further reduce drag around the wing.

Boeing said the 2009 PIP provided a 1% fuel burn improvement and an annual reduction of CO2 emissions of more than 3,000,000lb compared to the first 777-200s, 777-200ERs and 777-300s.

777-300ER Aerodynamic Optimisation

After the 2009 PIP, Boeing engineers turned their attention to improving the 777-300ER, 777-200LR and 777 Freighter. Changes for these models in three areas – aerodynamics, weight, and the GE Aviation GE90-115B turbofan engines – were subsequently introduced with a PIP announced in 2015.

One of the most important aerodynamic changes in this PIP was the deletion of the rear fuselage tailskid. Terry Beazhold, vice president and chief engineer for the Boeing 777X, told the author a new control law for the fly-by-wire flight control system (FCS) was developed. This software senses the location of the aft fuselage relative to the runway. If the system detects a potential tail strike it commands the elevators to generate nose-down pitch to prevent the tail striking the ground (see Three Hundred ER for more details). The software enabled Boeing to remove the tailskid and improve aerodynamic efficiency around the rear fuselage.

Another aerodynamic change introduced in the 2015 PIP was a divergent trailing edge. This involved adding a device to the underside of the wing outboard of the ailerons. This device increases the camber (or the asymmetry between a wing's top and bottom surfaces), which in turn increases airflow over the wing.

The divergent trailing edge is indicative of Boeing's wider design philosophy for the wings on its widebody aircraft, which is to maximise airflow over the aerofoil. The same philosophy explains why the 777 and the 787 have raked wingtips rather than the wingtip fences or winglets favoured by competitor Airbus.

Wind tunnel and computational fluid dynamics analysis of the wing indicated there was an opportunity to reduce drag in other areas. The aerodynamic changes in the 2015 PIP additionally involved smoothing out the inboard flap track fairings using what Beazhold described as a "tighter wrap" of the fairing into the wing.

IMPROVING

The divergent trailing edge is indicative of Boeing's wider design philosophy for the wings on its widebody aircraft, which is to maximise airflow over the aerofoil.

Attention was also paid to cutting drag on the fuselage. Beazhold said: "Believe it or not, with all those windows, a little step, a little mismatch between the window and the skin creates drag. We redesigned it to provide a much more consistent, flush window-to-skin interface."

Further drag reduction was achieved around the tail. "We found we could reduce drag by designing a better seal to close out some of the gaps around the elevator and the horizontal stabiliser," Beazhold said. The pitch trim software logic in the FCS was also revised, enabling the elevator to augment the stabiliser trim during the cruise to cut drag.

Reduced Weight

The second element of the 2015 PIP involved modifying the 777-300ER's structure to reduce weight by changing the side of the fuselage body and the architecture of the crown area (the space inside the aircraft above the cabin beneath the aircraft skin).

New lighter insulation blankets, lighter duct insulation, the adoption of lower-density (therefore lighter) fluid for the hydraulics, and lighter wheel and brake systems and tyres were also introduced.

Boeing told the author the lighter insulation blankets have saved 300lb in weight, the new duct insulation has saved 115lb, the revised wheel and brake systems 265lb and the lighter tyres 290lb. Removing the tailskid has also cut 325lb.

Overall, Boeing says a 777-300ER built today is now approximately 1,200lb lighter when compared to the first aircraft delivered to customers in 2004.

Engine Enhancements

The third part of the 2015 PIP concerned improvements to the GE90-115B engines equipping 777-300ERs, 777-200LRs and 777Fs.

The GE90 turbofan was developed by manufacturer GE Aviation specifically for the 777; it was the first commercial aircraft engine to use carbon fibre composite fan blades. The engine achieved 40 million hours of operational use in 2014, just four years after it passed the 20 million hours' mark.

The GE90 has proven to be highly efficient and reliable. The company says fuel burn on the 115,000lb-rated GE90-115B developed for the 777-300ER proved to be 3.6% better than what had been committed to during development and that the variant has a dispatch reliability of 99.8%.

GE Aviation continually invested in the GE90-115B following its service entry, spending $50 million annually on component improvements, so with this background of continued investment it was little wonder the company worked on improvements to the engine as part of the 2015 PIP.

The resulting Fuel Burn Upgrade package for the GE90-115B consists of several enhancements, drawing on technologies developed for the company's next-generation GEnx and Passport engines.

A GE Aviation spokesman said the package included adjusting the GE90-115B fan module's aerodynamics to smooth the flow path and reduce drag and modifying the high pressure compressor stage one blisk to improve efficiency. A new high pressure turbine (HPT) Active Clearance Control (ACC) manifold was introduced to provide tighter HPT tip clearance during the cruise, the HPT shroud grind was optimised to tighten the average tip-to-shroud clearances, and the low pressure turbine nozzle changed to improve efficiency. Lastly, an improved core compartment cooling valve with better reliability was introduced to improve cruise performance.

In addition to the three key upgrade areas of aerodynamics, weight and engines, Boeing also included a series of optional cabin upgrades in the 2015 PIP. These comprise lightweight galleys, space-saving lavatories and straightened aft seat tracks (together enabling operators to add up to 14 more seats), premium window shades, LED lighting, forward cabin noise improvements and an enhanced Door 2 entry.

The Numbers

Boeing claims that should 777-300ER, 777-200LR and 777F operators introduce all the key aerodynamics, weight reduction measures and engine changes of the 2015 PIP, they will see at least a 2% reduction in fuel burn per trip and a 5% reduction in per-seat costs compared to older 777 variants. The GE spokesman told the author the improvements to the GE90-115B account for about 0.5% of the 2% fuel burn saving.

ABOVE • BOEING

TOP RIGHT • AIRTEAMIMAGES/ MATTHIEU DOUHAIRE

BOTTOM RIGHT • EMIRATES

The 2015 PIP is available not just as the standard configuration for the 777-300ER and 777F, but also as retrofits for in-service aircraft. In July 2016 Boeing announced Qatar Airways as the launch customer for the PIP. The airline planned to upgrade all 43 (it had 91 by March 2024) of its 777s.

The GE Aviation spokesman added: "GE Aviation is also offering an engine upgrade kit with the HPT ACC manifold and an optional core compartment cooling valve that can be installed during a routine shop visit. About 1,800 GE90-115B engines can benefit from the package."

Link to the 777X

With the current-series Triple Seven the design baseline for the 777X, Beazhold emphasised the technology initially developed for the 777-300ER has nevertheless contributed to the new generation.

He said: "The 777X configuration tended to want the tailskid back on, so our flight scientists and flight controls team went about developing a more sophisticated control law that would perform an electronic, virtual tailskid. Our starting point was the [tailskid technology used on the] 777-300ER."

However, in a repeat of what happened in the 2009 PIP when 777-300ER technology was rolled into earlier aircraft, the current-series Triple Sevens have benefited from work under way on the newer models too; some of the improvements in the 2015 PIP were actually developed for the 777X first.

Beazhold explained: "For example, the divergent trailing edge was technology our flight sciences were developing [for the 777X]. When we started looking at the higher performance and technology of that aerodynamic shape it became apparent we could do something very similar on the 777-300ER."

This is indicative of Boeing's overall approach to designing and developing airliners. Beazhold said: "A lot of developments show up on different models at different times; we're really looking at how we continuously improve our whole family. There's a lot of cross-development between the different models."

Another example of this crossover is the divergent trailing edge development on the 777-300ER, which provided the basis not just for the 777X but also for the stretched 787-10 variant of the Dreamliner.

ECO-DRIVE

The Boeing ecoDemonstrator Programme explores new technologies and processes to reduce emissions and noise, improve airlines' efficiency and to help meet environmental and technology innovation goals.

The project was launched in 2011 and is intended to move ideas through development and into service more quickly by test-flying them. Five aircraft have been used as testbeds so far. The first was American Airlines' 737-800 N897NN (c/n 33318) in 2012, followed in 2014 by Boeing's own in-house 787-8 Dreamliner N7874 (c/n 40693). Next came 757-233 N757ET (c/n 24627) in 2015, then Embraer's in-house E170 test aircraft, PP-XJB (c/n 17000003), in 2016 followed by FedEx 777 Freighter N878FD (c/n 40684) in 2018, and 777-200 N772ET (c/n 29747) in 2019.

In September 2018, Jeanne Yu, Boeing Commercial Airplanes' director of environmental performance, told the author: "We've found the ecoDemonstrator [various] aircraft have really helped us innovate and explore. We've now tested 108 different technologies. I'd say close to a third of them have transitioned onto products, a third of them are on their way [to a product] and a third of them we've accomplished the learning and we've started work."

Doug Christensen, director of the ecoDemonstrator programme, told the author: "We use the ecoDemonstrators to bring some of these really breakthrough technologies onto our products really quickly."

One technology initially tested on the ecoDemonstrator and which subsequently found its way to a new aircraft was the winglet tested on the 2012 ecoDemonstrator, which went directly into the design of the Advanced Technology Winglet subsequently integrated on the 737 MAX family.

2018 ecoDemonstrator

Each phase of the ecoDemonstrator is a partnership with other organisations from around the industry. Partners involved in the programme to date have included airlines such as American Airlines and TUI, delivery services company FedEx, original equipment manufacturers like Embraer and Rolls-Royce, systems suppliers such as Rockwell Collins and the public bodies NASA and the Federal Aviation Administration.

Yu said: "Collaboration has been key. Working with partners to raise the overall level of technology innovation and knowledge has helped us go faster."

The 2018 ecoDemonstrator once again saw Boeing team up with several partners. FedEx supplied the 777F used as the testbed, and other parties involved included the Japan Aerospace Exploration Agency (JAXA), Safran and Embraer. In all, 37 technologies were tested aboard the Triple Seven spanning propulsion, materials, flight deck enhancements and efficient flight operations.

The 777F involved in the ecoDemonstrator was only delivered to FedEx in October 2017 and returned to Boeing in January 2018 for outfitting with the sensors and parts being tested. The aircraft flew as the ecoDemonstrator for around three months before being stripped of all test equipment and returned to FedEx in June 2018 to resume its normal freighter operations.

Thrust Reverser

One key technology tested on the ecoDemonstrator 777F was a new, Boeing-designed thrust reverser. Turbofan engine fan sizes are getting larger to provide more thrust, but this means the other engine components such as nacelles, cowlings and thrust reversers are also becoming larger.

Christensen said: "We have to find a way to keep them smaller; they can't just grow along with the fan diameter," because of course larger parts add weight and create drag.

For the 2018 ecoDemonstrator Boeing developed a prototype of a new, more compact thrust reverser, which uses some thermoplastic parts to cut weight and works with less hardware to reduce drag while the thruster is

• *Boeing 777-200 N772ET was the sixth testbed aircraft used for the ecoDemonstrator programme during the 2019 trials.* BOEING

Triple Seven
ecoDemonstrator

During the first two quarters of 2018, Boeing's ecoDemonstrator programme used a FedEx 777F to test new materials, systems, and engine technologies. **Mark Broadbent** reports.

ECO-DRIVE

not deployed. Christensen said: "We demonstrated on this aircraft the ability to configure the new thrust reverser to a General Electric GE90 engine [the 777's engine] and test it to make sure it had the same stopping power as a conventional thrust reverser."

N878FD was also fitted with a complete electrical channel supplied by Safran Electrical and Power, encompassing electric power generation and distribution systems, engine and aircraft wiring and electric fans.

Safran said: "Through strong collaboration with the Boeing team, Safran Electrical and Power designed and developed one of the fastest flight-worthy electrical channels for civil aircraft. This solution is unique in the market and allows future optimisation of the full aircraft electrical system."

According to Safran, the system has a single distribution panel managing all functions for control, protection, monitoring and recording of the aircraft's electrical network, and an electrical fan for cooling and cabin ventilation. Safran claims a variable-frequency geared power generator on the system reduces thermal losses by 60% and saves 15% in weight compared to the existing power-generation system on the 777.

Yu said: "[Safran] had planned to work with us over a four-year period to develop a capability to help us be more energy-efficient with regard to loads on the engine. They actually shortened their programme from four years to 18 months because of the ecoDemonstrator Programme."

The 777 ecoDemonstrator was responsible for a significant first: it was the first commercial airliner to fly using only alternative fuel. Biofuel demonstrations typically go up to 50% biofuel blended with conventional Jet A-1, but the FedEx 777 flew with 100% biofuel for some of its test flights.

Materials

The aircraft carried an additively-manufactured tail fin cap with NASA-integrated components. Christensen explained: "A part in the auxiliary power unit compartment was 3-D printed out of titanium. Not only is it lighter and a more efficient design, it's also about waste.

"We talk about the buy-to-fly ratio, the amount of material required to buy the amount of material that flies. We took a part that's normally milled from a block of titanium that has a 10:1 buy-to-fly ratio, and we printed that part using additive manufacturing that has a 2:1 buy-to-fly ratio. That's an 80% reduction in the titanium used for that part."

Boeing said it is, "always looking for ways to reduce manufacturing waste or use recycled material and testing methods for reusing manufacturing by-products and bringing the material back as high-value materials for new aircraft". To this end, the 777 ecoDemonstrator flew with a part made with recycled titanium, a

> The Boeing ecoDemonstrator Programme explores new technologies and processes to reduce emissions and noise, improve airlines' efficiency and to help meet environmental and technology innovation goals.

ABOVE • *The 777F approaches an inflatable pylon used during the ground tests of the Surface Operations and Collision Avoidance System at a wintry Glasgow Airport in Montana.* BOEING

TOP LEFT • *The LIDAR sensors search out ten statute miles ahead of the aircraft to find the location of any clear air turbulence.* BOEING

BOTTOM LEFT • *A more compact thrust reverser which uses some thermoplastic parts to cut weight was a key part tested in the ecoDemonstrator.* BOEING

RIGHT • *FedEx loaned 777 Freighter N878FD (c/n 40684) for the 2018 ecoDemonstrator.* BOEING/JOHN D PARKER

technology developed by Boeing in Russia and integrated on the aircraft in collaboration with Embraer.

Flight Operations

The ecoDemonstrator programme's efforts to improve environmental performance do not just involve aircraft parts, but also ways of improving the efficiency of flight operations.

A synthetic instrument landing system (ILS) was tested in the 2018 edition. Traditional ILS uses a radio beam transmitted from the ground, but Christensen said: "It can be trouble, it can go down or get blocked by other aircraft."

By contrast, synthetic ILS uses satellite information in the form of GPS signals to create the approach line for the aircraft's systems. Christensen explained: "It uses a GPS-based system to position the aircraft just like it would an ILS beam. The pilot sees the same indications [on the flight deck], the only difference is the indicator is using the satellite rather than the ILS beam. It's not affected by weather, by things going on at the airport. It allows operators to have a more consistent way of getting into the airport."

Boeing says the improved accuracy provided by the satellite-based data could enable tighter spacing between aircraft on approach and therefore more efficient operations for both airlines and airports, especially at peak times.

Surfing the Wake

When an aircraft flies, additional lift is created in the air by the vortex it leaves behind it. Christensen said: "You actually get free lift from the aircraft ahead of you. It's like what the birds do, there's efficiencies from flying behind that lead."

The 2018 ecoDemonstrator tested a new prediction algorithm to detect the wake turbulence left by an aircraft flying ahead. This algorithm uses a surveillance function provided by Aviation Communication and Surveillance Systems (ACSS), a joint venture between L3 and Thales.

N878FD was flown behind another FedEx 777F. Christensen said: "We demonstrated the ability to predict where the wake is from and then position the aircraft safely and 'surf' the wake to reduce fuel burn."

This was the first demonstration of the Boeing-developed algorithm. Christensen said: "Part of the testing and analysis is working out where's the best position [to ride the wave] and how can we position the aircraft. Depending upon where you position yourself on that wave you could get a five to ten per cent improvement in fuel burn."

Technology improving awareness about the positioning of airliners

ECO-DRIVE

LEFT • *The Boeing 777F returned to regular service with FedEx after the ecoDemonstrator trials concluded.* BOEING

RIGHT • *N878FD undertook some test flights powered by 100% biofuel.*

BOTTOM LEFT • BOEING

in the airways would clearly assist in efficient navigation and route management, so, separate to the wake turbulence work, the ecoDemonstrator 777F was also used to acquire data now being used to develop the Airborne Collision Avoidance System X standard (ACAS X). This next enhancement of the TCAS II (Traffic Collision and Avoidance System) standard is designed to enhance flight safety, improve navigation aids, and provide efficient route management and fuel optimisation. Another surveillance function supplied by ACSS supported this work.

Clear Air Turbulence

The ecoDemonstrator 777F also tested a prototype clear air turbulence (CAT) detection system developed by Boeing in partnership with JAXA.

This system uses LIDAR: pulsed laser light illuminates the target to measure the reflection with a sensor to generate the distance to the target, in this case turbulent air. It searches out ten statute miles ahead of the aircraft, which JAXA says is the longest range on any CAT sensor yet developed, to find the location of any upcoming CAT that conventional weather radars fail to identify. Importantly, Christensen added, "it shows not only the strength of the turbulence, but also a countdown of when it's coming in and how soon it'll hit."

The system, Yu said, gives the crew about 70 seconds' warning of the turbulence ahead, enabling the crew to turn on the seatbelt sign and warn passengers and crew to sit down and avoid any potential injury caused by the bumps.

Christensen said: "We spent a full day out in Kansas and found some weather that would give us some clear air turbulence. We flew into the turbulent air and watched the system predict it, counting down to when the aircraft would hit. It was quite amazing how accurate the system was in its predictions.

He added that JAXA is now working on how to integrate such a CAT detection system into current flight displays. The system installed in the ecoDemonstrator 777F weighed 184lb, which JAXA said is equivalent to one passenger with one bag, so a small weight penalty. JAXA believes the system could potentially reduce injuries caused by turbulence by 60%.

SOCAS

Another feature tested on the ecoDemonstrator 777F was the Surface Operations and Collision Avoidance

System (SOCAS), designed to help a flight crew identify if there are any obstacles – other aircraft, buildings, ground operations vehicles, people – in the way of the aircraft while it is taxiing on the ground in poor weather.

Data from a radar sensor and imagery from a video camera are combined to generate a 'map' of the environment surrounding the aircraft, with all the surrounding objects, cars, buildings, and aircraft modelled. This map enables the SOCAS to 'sense' what is around the aircraft and identify any potential collisions. The system then notifies the crew that an object is in the way.

A fire truck and a large inflatable and moveable pylon were used at Glasgow Airport in Montana to test the ability of the SOCAS to detect the obstacles and provide warnings about them.

Looking Ahead

With the ecoDemonstrator Programme having tested so many technologies in just a few years, it is perhaps unsurprising to learn that the programme continues.

Yu confirmed: "Our leaders want us to accelerate and increase the frequency of our test platforms. We are looking at a whole list of technologies that have been proposed and we're in the process of pairing-off [technologies] with the right platform and right timing and deciding what platforms we need."

2019 ecoDemonstrator

In 2019, Boeing's ecoDemonstrator programme used a 777-200 N772ET (c/n 29747) as testbed trialling 50 technologies during the autumn, including a trip to Frankfurt International Airport, Germany, where the ecoDemonstrator's technology mission was presented to government officials, industry representatives and STEM students.

Tests conducted in 2019 included how better to share digital information between air traffic control agencies, the flight deck and an airline's operations centre to optimise routing efficiency and safety. Also, part of the testing is an electronic flight bag application that uses next-generation communications to provide rerouting information to pilots automatically when weather conditions change, and cameras to provide more passengers with a view outside the aircraft.

The all-important passenger connectivity was also trialled using a standard for networked cabins called iCabin that Boeing says, "makes galleys and lavatories smart and monitors cabin conditions such as temperature and humidity to facilitate automatic adjustments".

To reduce emissions and demonstrate viability, most test flights were flown on sustainable aviation fuel.

Since Boeing launched the ecoDemonstrator programme, 250 technologies have been tested, of which more than a third, the company says, "have transitioned to implementation".

Among technologies now in use are iPad apps that provide real-time information to pilots, enabling them to reduce fuel use and emissions; custom approach path information to reduce community noise; and a camera system on the 777X that will help pilots avoid ground obstacles. The latter was tested in the 2018 ecoDemonstrator edition involving the 777F.

In 2020, Boeing partnered with Etihad Airways in using a 787-10 Dreamliner to test systems designed to reduce emissions and noise, and, in 2023, Boeing used its ecoDemonstrator 777-200ER to test 19 technologies including sustainable wall panels, fibre-optic fuel quantity sensors and a Smart Maps feature to support safe taxi operations using contextual airport data.

BRITISH AIRWAYS

British Airways
Triple Sevens

Boeing's 777 has proved popular with British Airways – it has already operated four different variants and recently placed an order for a new variant of the big twin. **Bob O'Brien** looks at the Triple Seven's career with Britain's national carrier.

AIRTEAMIMAGES/
COLIN PARKER

In December 1988, Boeing invited several of its customers, including British Airways, to take part in talks to define an all-new design intended to replace the ageing fleets of McDonnell Douglas DC-10s and Lockheed TriStars then in service with many of the world's major airlines.

Following an exhaustive process, Boeing eventually settled on a new design in 1990 and named it the 777. Though similar in appearance to the 767, the first variant was just 20ft shorter than the 747-300 and shared the latter's wing span and fuselage width.

The 777 was officially launched in October 1990 with an order from United Airlines for 34, plus options for the same number. This would be Boeing's first fully fly-by-wire airliner and featured a glass cockpit.

First Order

In August 1991, the British Airways board authorised the purchase of five 777-200s and ten of the 777-200IGW (increased gross weight) variant which was designated 777-236ER with the British carrier and procured to carry more passengers. Options were also taken for ten 200ERs.

The first flight of the 777-200 took place on June 12, 1994 and was carried out by N777UA, which later entered service with United Airlines. This variant had a range of 5,240nm with max payload. The first example for British Airways, G-ZZZA, took to the air on February 2 the following year. Boeing's designations had previously assigned '36' as the customer code for British Airways, so officially the type was a 777-236. This applied to all the subsequent models entering service with British Airways, however this naming system has now been dropped and will not be used for the 777-9s ordered by British Airways.

Before this aircraft was delivered it visited Heathrow over April 20-21, 1995 (registered N77779) to help familiarise British Airways staff with the new type. Along with G-ZZZB it took part in the 777's flight test programme.

The first 777 delivered to British Airways arrived at Heathrow on

BRITISH AIRWAYS

November 11, 1995. Six days later the same aircraft, G-ZZZC, flew the inaugural scheduled service for the carrier on the Heathrow to Muscat, Oman route, via Dubai. It was named Sir Charles Edward Kingsford Smith in honour of the aviation pioneer. Only five 777 aircraft, G-ZZZA to G-ZZZE have been named, all after famous aviators.

In British Airways service the 777-200's cabin is divided into three sections: 17 seats in First Class, 70 for Club World and 148 in World Traveller (economy) with each class served by its own galley. The aircraft was the first to receive what the carrier refers to as 'High Comfort Seats' for cabin crew who also have use of three passenger seats at the back of the World Traveller cabin. Initially, the crew complement for a 200 series was two pilots, a cabin service director, three pursers (later reduced to two), and eight cabin crew.

For the remainder of the 1995-1996 winter season, three aircraft, G-ZZZC, G-ZZZD and G-ZZZE only served Cairo and Paris CDG to build up flight crew hours on the type.

In September 1996, the airline ordered a further three 777-236ERs. All of them were delivered in March 1998. At the time British Airways also held options for a further 17 200ERs.

ETOPS

The 777 received approval for 180 minutes extended twin-operations (ETOPS) in October 1996. This allowed the type to fly routes that were three hours' flying time from a suitable diversion airport should an engine fail and enabled British Airways to introduce it on flights to the United States.

As well as destinations such as Riyadh and Jeddah, the 777 was also used on three rotations a day to Paris.

The first 777-236ER, G-VIIC, was delivered in February 1997 with the uprated GE90-92B(85B) engine, capable of producing 92,000lb of thrust but operated at a reduced rate of 90,000lb. These aircraft were configured to carry 32 more passengers for a total of 267 comprising 14 in First Class, 56 in Club World and 197 in World Traveller. This layout meant the previously spacious World Traveller galley (compared with the other two sections) in the 200 had to be halved in size to accommodate more toilets.

The variant proved well suited to destinations on the United States' East Coast, Middle East and India.

Five ER options were confirmed in June 1997 to operate from the airline's base at Gatwick to – among other places – Bermuda, Dallas, Atlanta, and Accra in Ghana. The first British Airways 777 service from Gatwick was flown by G-VIIA, departing to Bermuda on February 3, 1998. With the airline growing its network, a fleet of seven 777s was required to cover flights from Gatwick in that year's summer season and so extra examples were transferred from Heathrow. This number served at the West Sussex airport until the effects of the air travel industry caused by the COVID-19 pandemic struck.

A further five ERs were purchased in May 1998, taking the total on firm order to 29 airframes. Three that arrived in May the following year were delivered to Gatwick to take over flying for the Airline Management Ltd (AML) contract, a joint venture company established by British Airways and the Flying Colours group. The new airliners replaced three former British Caledonian Airways DC-10-30s. These 777s operated flights to Mexico, Cuba, Jamaica, and

The first Boeing 777-200 for British Airways, G-ZZZA, took to the air on February 2, 1995. Boeing's designations had previously assigned '36' as the customer code for British Airways, so officially the type was a 777-236.

AIRTEAMIMAGES/
FLORENT
LACRESSONNNIERE

the Dominican Republic under the British Airways banner with pilots drawn from the main triple seven fleet, and the cabin crew from AML. The contract was served by G-VIIO, G-VIIP and G-VIIR, fitted with a two-class configuration capable of carrying 383 passengers (28 in Club World and 355 in World Traveller). These aircraft were among the seven examples at Gatwick operating holiday flights in various cabin configurations.

Towards the end of the 1990s the initial six 777-236ERs had their cabin layout altered, with First Class removed in favour of adding further 76 World Traveller seats.

In August 1998, British Airways ordered 16 777-236ERs powered by Rolls-Royce Trent 895 engines (rated at 95,000lb) which could fly 7,730nm with max payload. The aircraft were delivered in a three-class configuration with sufficient range to carry a full load of passengers and cargo to Hong Kong, Beijing, and Rio de Janeiro. They had the same galley configurations as the previous two variants, a small galley in the front of the aircraft to cater for First Class, a mid-galley adjacent to door 2 for Club World and a small galley at the rear to cater for World Traveller. Due to their use on long-distance flights, Boeing incorporated crew rest areas within the initial design. A sleeping area for two pilots was created at the rear of First Class on the right side requiring the removal of two passenger seats. Cabin crew rest quarters were originally installed below D3R (door 3 right), accessed via a small stairway to a sleeping compartment within the hold. However, the loss of belly cargo capacity led the airline to move this area into the upper fuselage ceiling above D3R, accommodating eight bunks and two rest seats. The first of these extended-range variants, G-YMMA, was delivered on January 7, 2000.

It was one of these aircraft, G-YMMM, that is the only example from the British Airways 777 fleet being written off. On January 17, 2008, this aircraft was operating British Airways 038 from Beijing when it touched down inside the airport boundary but short of Runway 27L. Thanks to the efforts of the crew, the passengers were evacuated successfully. The aircraft was dismantled on site and taken away to be parted out. Among the 'probable causal factors' the official crash report stated: "Accreted ice from within the fuel system released, causing a restriction to the engine fuel flow at the face of the FOHE [fuel oil heat exchanger], on both of the engines." It added that: "Certification requirements, with which the aircraft and engine fuel systems had to comply, did not take account of this phenomenon as the risk was unrecognised at that time."

Cabin configurations for the extended-range version of the aircraft consists of 12 seats in First Class, 48 in Club World, 32 in World Traveller Plus and 127 in World Traveller. The first seven 777-236ERs for the airline's leisure routes were configured differently, with 48 seats in Club World, 24 in World Traveller Plus and 203 in World Traveller.

These aircraft served Bangkok, Buenos Aires, Montreal and some of the southern Indian destinations, whilst also often being ferried to Gatwick when extra capacity was required or substitutes needed for aircraft undergoing maintenance.

777-300ERs

British Airways had started to retire some of its early Boeing 747-400s in

BRITISH AIRWAYS

AIRTEAMIMAGES/
JOHN KILMER

2008 and the airline felt the 777-300ER was an ideal replacement. In 2008 an initial six were ordered, with the first example to enter the fleet, G-STBA, delivered on September 7, 2010. Powered by two GE90-115B1 engines, each rated at 115,540lb of thrust, the aircraft has a range of 7,830nm with max payload. Four classes of seating comprise 14 in First Class, 56 in Club World, 44 in World Traveller Plus and 185 in World Traveller.

A 777-336ER has a crew of 15 – two pilots, one cabin service director, two pursers and ten cabin crew. The rest area for pilots, featuring two bunk beds, each with an in-flight entertainment system, was relocated above the cabin adjacent to D1L. Cabin crew were allocated a large ten-bunk unit in the roof area above D5L.

The type was placed on the prestigious 'Kangaroo' route linking London with Sydney via Singapore.

British Airways decided to increase capacity on the Gatwick-based 777-236ERs from 280 seats to 332 seats by changing its nine-abreast layout in World Traveller to a ten-abreast arrangement. Consequently, the new cabin has 32 seats in Club World, 52 in World Traveller Plus and 252 in World Traveller, and features a new Panasonic in-flight entertainment system.

On February 28, 2019, British Airways' parent company International Airlines Group announced an order for 18 Boeing 777-9s (with options for another 24), powered by the GE9X engines and seating for 425 passengers – intended to replace the remaining 747s.

As of spring, 2024, the British Airway's fleet of Boeing 777s sits at 59 aircraft: 43 777-200s (comprising both 777-236s and 777-236ERs) and 16 777-300s.

www.key.aero 47

FREIGHTERS

Boeing 777 Freighters

Most jet freighters are converted from older passenger aircraft, but Boeing took a gamble on the market being ready for a new-build freighter version of the 777, and has met with considerable success, as detailed by **Barry Lloyd.**

In response to requests from some of Boeing's most important customers, in 2004 the manufacturer set up a working group involving 20 airlines and cargo operators, with a view to designing and producing an all-freight version of the Boeing 777. It was envisaged as a replacement for cargo versions of the McDonnell Douglas DC-10 and MD-11, and Boeing 747, 757 and 767 freighters. A launch order from Air France for five 777Fs in May 2005 got the ball rolling, with the type's inaugural flight taking place on July 14, 2008. The first example was delivered to Air France on February 19 the following year.

The 777F can carry a 242,500lb payload and has a maximum take-off weight of 766,000lb. Twenty-seven standard pallets can be accommodated on the main deck, with space for ten more in the lower cargo hold. Additionally, there is room for 600ft3 of bulk freight in the aft belly hold. It can accommodate various types and sizes of pallets. Many cargo operators carry bloodstock, usually horses being transported between race meetings in different countries or being brought to and from stud. For these operations,

A launch order from Air France for five 777Fs in May 2005 got the ball rolling, with the type's inaugural flight taking place on July 14, 2008. The first example was delivered to Air France on February 19 the following year.

there is a small section known as the supernumerary area near the forward door that can be used by handlers. It has four business-sized seats, a galley and toilet facilities plus two bunks. With a max payload range of 5,400nm the aircraft can fly further than the 747-8F. The aircraft includes features of the 777-200LR, marketed as the Worldliner, such as the basic airframe and engines, but incorporates the fuel capacity of the larger 777-300ER.

Standard features across the 777 series include a state-of-the-art flight deck, fly-by-wire controls and an advanced wing design that includes raked wing tips. In order for it to operate in an all-cargo configuration, additional strengthening of the main deck floor and other areas, including a fixed cargo barrier to the forward area of the aircraft, were also introduced. The main deck cargo door is fitted at the rear of the aircraft and is 12ft 2in wide and 9ft 8in high.

The 777F uses the same engines as its passenger-carrying stablemates, the GE Aviation GE90-110B. Its noise footprint is below that mandated by the Chapter 4 noise requirement – a useful selling point when so much of its activity takes place during the hours of darkness and close to heavily populated areas.

Expanding Markets

The growth in the air cargo market has, to a large degree, been a result of the growth of e-commerce, together with the year-round demand for supplies of fresh fruit and vegetables. In addition, those manufacturing companies that use the just-in-time delivery system require reliable jets. The retirement of freighters such as the 767 and DC-10 has also meant that operators have been forced to look for replacements.

Increasing world trade is also fuelling demand for freighter conversions and such is the level of competition within their own markets that package couriers in particular are always looking for lower-cost alternatives to buying new aircraft. Offering revamped versions of the 777-200ERs would expand Boeing's catalogue of freighters, but could potentially risk sales of new aircraft, which are significantly more expensive. Talk of a 200ER freighter programme has been around for more

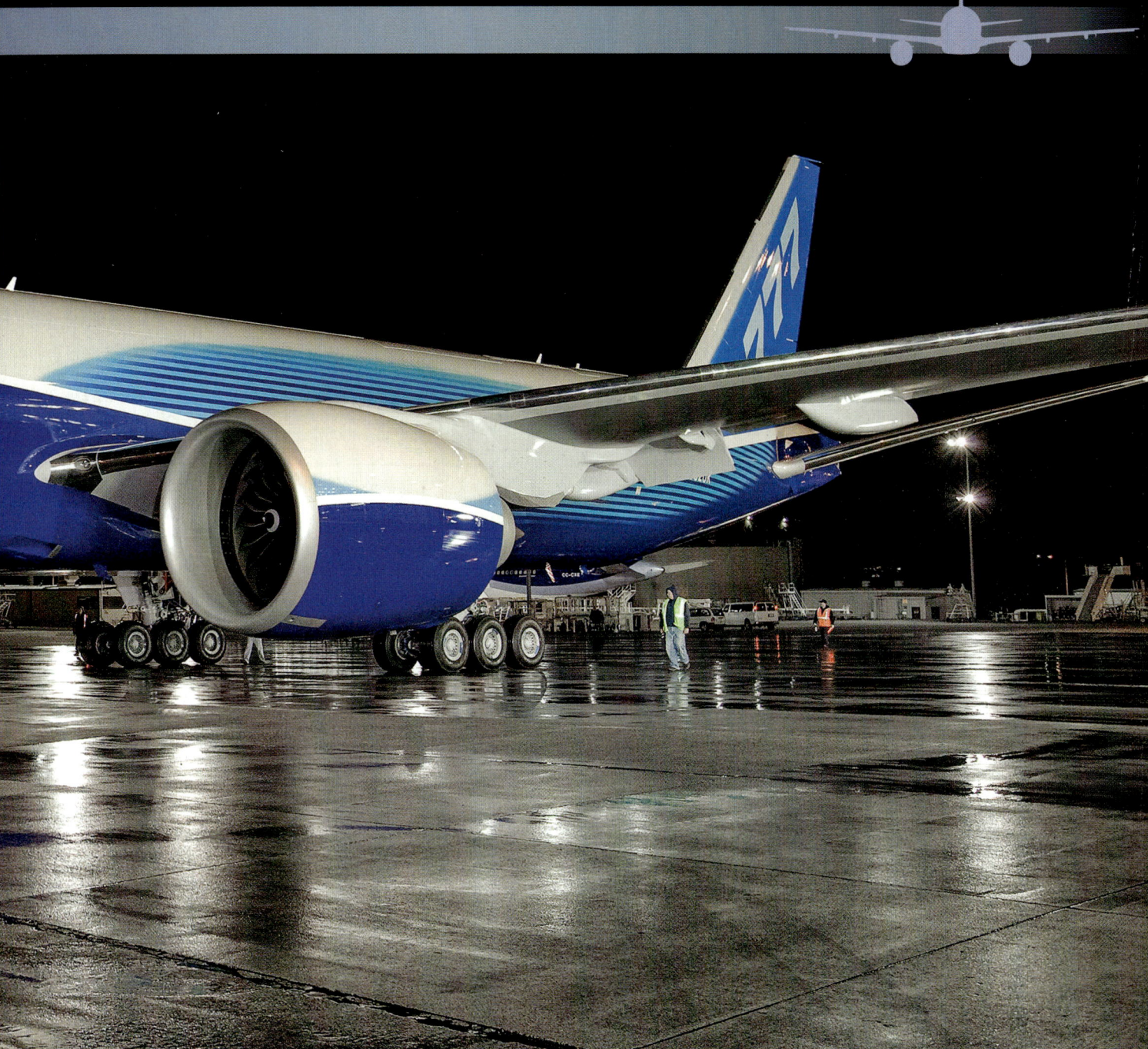

ABOVE • BOEING

than a decade, but the main problem is the cost of conversion. One of the biggest areas of work and so cost, is the requirement to strengthen the cabin floor beams to accommodate heavily-laden pallets. As the potential market expands, several companies are offering customers passenger-to-freighter (P2F) conversions.

The Bedek Division of Israel Aerospace Industries, which has considerable experience in performing freighter conversions, has begun a programme to create 777-300 freighters, using manufacturer-provided drawings, with Emirates announced as a customer in 2021 (see page 53). The 'Big Twin' aircraft made its first public appearance in late 2023, at the Dubai Air Show. IAI has conversion partners in both Arizona and South Korea to carry out this programme and expects certification in summer 2024.

Hold Cargo

Passenger 777s also have an impressive cargo-carrying capacity. For example, the 300 variant has sufficient underfloor space for 50,700lb of cargo. This represents 25% more capacity than even the 747-8I, thus providing useful additional revenue to scheduled airline operators. An example of the volume of the 777 belly hold is that it can easily – and frequently does – accommodate a luxury sports car on a pallet. Not all freight needs to move between major cargo hubs and belly-loaded freight can be carried to destinations which are important, but do not have major cargo-handling facilities, or where there is insufficient requirement for pure freight services.

Deliveries of the 777F began in 2009, with 16 being delivered that year, rising to 22 in 2010. The type has so far been sold to 36 different operators. Customers have included the pure-cargo carriers, such as AeroLogic (a Lufthansa/DHL joint venture) and Southern Air. Many airlines have ordered passenger 777s, but also the freighter version – such as Emirates, Qatar Airways, Air Canada, China Southern Airlines, and Korean Air. Four leasing companies: Alatavair, Aerologic, GECAS, and Oak Hill/Avolon have also purchased 777Fs. By spring 2024, Boeing had orders for 319 777Fs of which 264 had been delivered.

With the 777X coming down the track, Boeing will no doubt be looking carefully to see if there is a viable economic market for further new 777Fs, or whether to close that part of the line. Whatever happens, 777 freighters will be plying the trade routes for many years to come.

www.key.aero 51

Fully fledged freighter

After a near 15 year career flying for Emirates, this Boeing 777-300ER swapped seats and suites for freight to become the first example of what's now been dubbed The Big Twin. **Dirk Grothe** provided a first look for *Airliner World*

Delivered new to the Dubai-based behemoth in December 2005, the 540th Boeing 777-300ER off the production line, A6-EBI (c/n 32785), spent the first 14 years of its life flying passengers all over the world. However, in its 15th and final year with Emirates, the jet would get a glimpse of its future as COVID-19 prompted the Middle Eastern carrier to reconfigure the airliner as a 'preighter', removing its seats to create additional cargo capacity while the world weathered the logistical storm created by the pandemic.

Having been returned to its lessor, General Electric Capital Aviation Services (GECAS), the twin-aisle jet was stored at Victorville's Southern California Logistics Airport in May 2021. However, with AerCap's acquisition of GECAS that November, its new owner identified a fresh role for the aircraft.

The Irish lessor, which had partnered with Israel Aerospace Industries (IAI) in launching a Boeing 777-300ER freighter conversion programme (nicknamed The Big Twin) in 2019, identified the aircraft – along with four other ex-Emirates jets – as ideal feedstock for the Tel Aviv conversion line.

It is anticipated that the installation of an aft cargo door, a new, strengthened cabin floor designed for a 100-ton payload and structural reinforcements around the cargo door will take around four to six months to complete. IAI is no stranger to freighter conversions, having undertaken around 60 projects on 737s, 747s and 767s previously. However, its Tel Aviv/Ben Gurion base will be supplemented by additional facilities at Etihad Engineering's Abu Dhabi headquarters

BELOW • *This Boeing 777-300ERSF, N778CK (c/n 32789), was the first example to undergo passenger to freighter conversion.*
AIRTEAMIMAGES.COM/YOCHAI

The first five examples of the 'Big Twin' to be converted are set to be leased to Kalitta Air

The Big Twin's strengthened cabin floor is designed for a 100-ton payload

ABOVE • *The Big Twin's strengthened cabin floor is designed for a 100-ton payload.* DIRK GROTHE

and at Incheon International Airport, South Korea.

The 777-300ERSF compares favourably to other widebody freighters, boasting a 25% larger cargo capacity – equivalent to an additional 18 tons – to the in-production Boeing 777F and 22% lower operating costs per ton compared to the 777-200LR-based jet. It also has a 9-ton advantage over the Boeing 747-400BCF while fuel consumption is 21% lower per ton, and its similar range means it is able to fly the popular Hong Kong to Anchorage freight route.

The first five examples of the 'Big Twin' to be converted are set to be leased to Kalitta Air. Currently, two airframes – N778CK (c/n 32789) and N779CK, the former A6-EBI – have been converted and are conducting flight test and certification work following the former's first post-conversion flight on March 23, 2023. The other three are all in the process of being converted. AerCap currently holds 20 firm orders and a further ten options for the 777-300ERSF, which equate to around a quarter of IAI's order book, which currently comprises 65 firm orders and more than 50 options. Once certified, Kalitta Air will become the launch operator when it receives the first of seven 777-300ERSFs leased from AerCap in early 2024. Emirates SkyCargo and EVA Air Cargo are also due to receive examples in the coming years.

ABOVE • *The first Boeing 777-300ER to undergo freighter conversion, N778CK (c/n 32789), receives its aft cargo door at IAI's Tel Aviv/Ben Gurion conversion facility.* ISRAEL AEROSPACE INDUSTRIES

BELOW • *Kalitta Air has signed for seven Boeing 777-300ERSFs on lease from AerCap. The first five of these will be former Emirates aircraft, with N779CK (c/n 32785) making somewhat of a homecoming when the jet appeared on static display at the 2023 Dubai Airshow held at DWC.* DIRK GROTHE

> IAI is no stranger to freighter conversions, having undertaken around 60 projects on 737s, 747s and 767s previously.

PIMA'S 777-200

"As the world's very first 777, B-HNL holds a very special place in the history of both our airline and that of commercial aviation, and we are very pleased it will now bring enjoyment to enthusiasts at its new home in Arizona." Cathay Pacific CEO Rupert Hogg

Pima's Boeing 777-200

Mark Ayton covers the donation and delivery of the first Boeing 777-200 ever built to the Tucson, Arizona-based Pima Air & Space Museum.

AIRTEAMIMAGES/COLIN PARKER

In late 2018, Cathay Pacific and Boeing donated the first Boeing 777 ever built to the Pima Air & Space Museum in Tucson, Arizona. The 777-200 aircraft (line number WA001, registered B-HNL) was flown from Cathay Pacific's base in Hong Kong to Davis-Monthan Air Force Base arriving there after a near 14-hour flight. B-HNL departed Hong Kong just after 12:20pm local time and arrived at Davis-Monthan at 11:14am on September 18, 2018.

Speaking to the press at the time, Cathay Pacific CEO Rupert Hogg said: "As the world's very first 777, B-HNL holds a very special place in the history of both our airline and that of commercial aviation, and we are very pleased it will now bring enjoyment to enthusiasts at its new home in Arizona.

"Our 777-200 aircraft have served us exceptionally well over the last two decades, and as we progressively retire these, we eagerly look forward to welcoming the state-of-the art 777-9s into our fleet," he added.

Boeing Commercial Airplanes president and CEO Kevin McAllister said: "Cathay Pacific has been instrumental in the tremendous success of the 777 programme. The airline contributed greatly to the aircraft's original design and has been one of its biggest ambassadors ever since. And now is a launch customer for the new 777X. We are thrilled to partner with Cathay on this donation to the museum as a way to share the remarkable story of the Boeing 777 for years come."

The aircraft (line number WA001 and later registered B-HNL) was rolled out of the Everett production facility on April 9, 1994 and made the type's maiden flight 64 days later. WA001 was used as a flight test aircraft throughout the 11-month flight test programme and remained with Boeing until it was sold to Cathay Pacific in 2000. Before delivery to the Hong Kong based carrier that December, as a condition of its sale, the aircraft's original Pratt & Whitney 4000 series engines were replaced with Rolls-Royce 800s fitted to new engine pylons. B-HNL remained in service with Cathay Pacific until its retirement in May 2018.

According to Boeing, in the 1990s, Cathay Pacific was one of a handful of airlines to provide input for the 777 during the design phase. This gave Hong Kong's home airline a unique opportunity to refine the aircraft's features to suit its needs. Among the requests were a cabin cross-section similar to the Boeing 747, a modern glass cockpit, fly-by-wire system, and lower operating costs.

The jet is now on permanent display at the museum.

JASDF 777-300ERs

Japan's Triple Sevens

Mark Ayton reviews the acquisition and operation of two Boeing 777-300ER aircraft by the Japanese Air Self Defense Force.

AIRTEAMIMAGES/
MATTHIEU DOUHAIRE

The first Boeing 777-3SBER for the Japan Air Self-Defense Force (JASDF) arrived at Chitose Air Base, home of the Special Air Transport Corps on August 17, 2018. Construction number 62439 and line number 1422 was delivered wearing the Boeing test registration N509BJ, but by August 30 it had been formally handed over to the JASDF with the serial number 80-1111; the second aircraft (80-1112) arrived at Chitose in December in advance of retirement of the organisation's 747-400s in March 2019.

Both 777s are assigned to the JASDF's Air Support Command based at Fuchu, Tokyo and operated by the 701 Hikotai, a unit within the Special Airlift Group based at Chitose Air Base, Hokkaido. Both 777s are used to transport the emperor, the imperial family, and prime ministerial entourages on visits around the world.

Dubbed as 'flying cabinet offices', the two 777 aircraft are also used to rescue and repatriate Japanese and other nationals overseas, for international disaster relief operations, and for peace co-operation and contribution activities (supporting coalition forces in combat zones). The squadron, 701st Hikotai, flew its first mission involving the evacuation and repatriation of Japanese nationals from Algeria between January 21 and 24, 2013.

On August 12, 2014, the Japanese Ministry of Defence awarded a maintenance contract for their 777-300 aircraft to ANA Holdings.

Conversion training of 777 in-flight personnel commenced at an ANA facility on May 15, 2017 followed on August 17, 2018 by the arrival of the first aircraft. The first overseas training operation, transporting 35 personnel from Haneda to Sydney, Australia took place between November 3-5, 2018.

Assumption of the Special Airlift Group's operational missions with the 777 took place between April 22 and April 29, 2019 when Prime Minister Shinzo Abe visited Paris, Rome, Vienna, Brussels, and Washington DC.

The two JASDF 777s, dubbed Japan's Air Force One and Two, are fitted with VIP rooms, executive compartments, and conference rooms.

JASDF maintenance crews fly on board the 777s to fix any maintenance issues and maintain the aircraft's availability. All in-flight crew are JASDF personnel who, among many things, weigh, and load VIP's luggage, provide in-flight food service and make announcements.

Safety, punctuality, and provision of comfort are the crew's main responsibilities for which timing is everything. According to the JASDF, VIP schedules are planned to the nearest minute and begin from the arrival of the aircraft; flight delay directly impacts the VIP's plans. On-time arrival is always required.

LUFTHANSA LUXURY

Positively Palatial

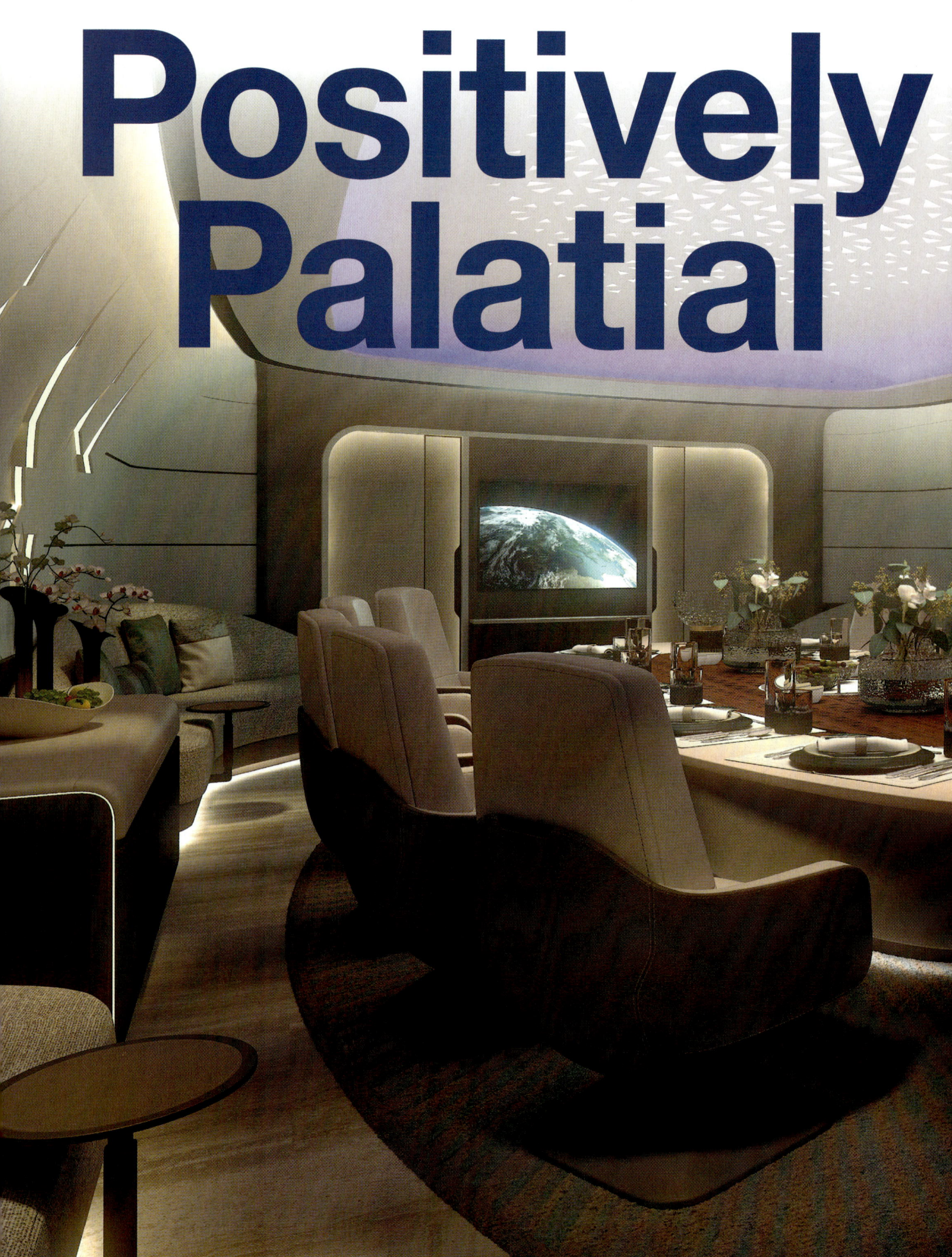

Lufthansa Technik's VVIP Boeing BBJ (or Boeing Business Jet) 777-9 concept is aimed squarely at the Middle East, as **Ian Harbison** discovered

To launch a new product for a particular world area might seem to be a bit risky but there is a clear logic for Lufthansa Technik, according to Wieland Timm, the company's Head of Sales for Special Mission Aircraft. Many of the current fleet of government and head of state aircraft in the region have been regular visitors to the Hamburg maintenance base over the years, so there is a familiarity and understanding on both sides.

However, these aircraft, particularly 747s, are ageing and need to be replaced in the not too distant future. The 777-9 is the largest production aircraft available, with its 350m² of floor space making it the perfect baseline for an interior that can provide private accommodation for the leader, public areas for dining or conferences and seating for supporting officials and staff.

While there have been earlier VVIP 777 concepts from other companies, Timm noted the 777-9 has a wider fuselage than the -300 and the doors are in different positions. This made it important to wait before starting work on the design and, as Lufthansa Technik is the first to use native aircraft data provided by Boeing, all dimensions and space are 100% accurate, ensuring the feasibility of the layout.

In addition, Lufthansa is the launch customer for the airline version, now expecting the first of 20 aircraft in 2025 after several delays. By the time the first airframe is available off the production line for VVIP conversion, Lufthansa Technik will have acquired all the necessary equipment, completed training and gained plenty of experience in looking after the type. Design of an actual layout will likely take around 16 months, with a conversion time of 14-16 months, and that is why, said Timm, the decision was made to launch the VVIP concept in 2023.

The concept – designed completely in house – was launched at EBACE, revealing the entrance to the principal passenger's quarters and the Majlis (Arabic for sitting room).

Some of those heads of state are also ageing and will be replaced in the near future, so the design

BELOW • *A view of the Majlis, looking forward, set up for dining. The wall-mounted petals have been moved to cover the windows while the light projection system is decorating the ceiling.*
ALL PHOTOS LUFTHANSA TECHNIK UNLESS STATED

LUFTHANSA LUXURY

The Airbus ACJ TwoTwenty: Versatility in Spades

In a further cabin development, Lufthansa Technik has unveiled a highly flexible design for the Airbus ACJ TwoTwenty to meet the needs of government and military operators. Based on the A220-100, it can provide transportation for VIPs and delegations with a high level of comfort and functionality as well as security and privacy. In addition, it can be reconfigured for the medical evacuation (medevac) role, which, the company says, is currently in particularly high demand.

At the front of the aircraft, there is a self-contained VIP cabin, with two conference seats, a table, a full double bed and an exclusive lavatory. An aft door leads to a conference area with seven seats, all fully certified for take-off and landing. A divider separates this from the large delegation area consisting of 12 Premium Economy Class (in a 2+2 layout) and 20 Economy Class seats (also in a 2+2 layout). Altogether, 41 passengers can travel in this configuration, significantly more than on conventional business jets but at comparable operating costs.

In the medevac role, up to eight stretchers can be installed in the delegation area to transport non-critical patients, or a pair of the company's Patient Transport Unit Next Generation (PTU NG) intensive care units can be installed for seriously ill patients. Mixed configurations with stretchers and PTU NGs are also possible.

With additional tanks, the Lufthansa Technik ACJ TwoTwenty configuration will have a range of up to 5,650nm (a 64% increase on the 3,450nm range for an A220-100 in airline configuration).

reflects newer cultural trends in the region, taking inspiration from 5* and 6* hotels, with more emphasis on fabric and less on gold and leather.

A forward entrance has a galley to one side, which is exclusive to the principal passenger. A curving passageway on the port side leads to the rest of the aircraft. The curve comes from the exterior wall of the master suite, which is enclosed in an elliptical cocoon and contains a bathroom and bedroom. A projection system from Diehl Aerospace, previously part of the Lufthansa Technik 'Explorer' concept in 2021, can fill the room with images or colours. Aft of the bedroom is a private eating/working area followed by the entrance area from the Majlis.

The Majlis features a central table, a reflection of the younger generation's preferences while working or eating, although four traditional divans, each with a small table, are in each corner. The seat and the central table will be able to rotate to face the divans and to move forward slightly. Hidden cupboards are installed close to the sidewalls to

ABOVE • *In this view of the Majlis, a chair at the central table has been rotated, allowing conversation with passengers sitting in one of four corner divan areas.*

LEFT • *A view of the Majlis, looking forward, set up for working. The wall-mounted petals have been moved to reveal the windows.*

BELOW • *A floor plan of the Boeing BBJ 777-9 concept design.*

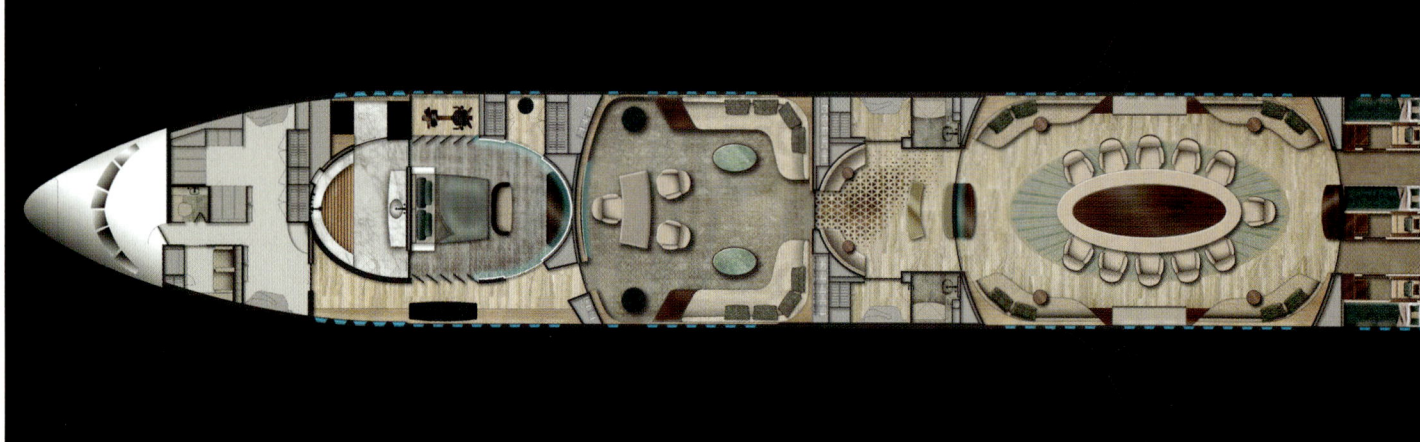

RIGHT • *A view, looking forward, of the reception area of the Majlis.*

RIGHT • *Another view of the reception area, with doors to the Majlis closed.*

maintain a clean look. This layout is made possible by the cabin width.

No window shades are fitted. Instead, moving petals can be adjusted electronically to provide the desired light levels. The geometric shapes are derived from modern Arabic design, and also form a screen for the light projection system.

The next section of the cabin has first class suites for the highest officials, then business class suites for the next level of staff and premium economy seats in the rear for the delegation. Toilets and a large galley are installed at the back.

Connectivity and IFE will be high end, Timm said. By the time an aircraft is available for conversion, the latest generation of equipment will offer ten times the data rate of current systems in service, combined with satcom antennae with reduced drag and improved performance. For IFE, two servers are likely to be fitted, as the principal passenger may need to access sensitive information.

Medical facilities are mandatory, and the company can incorporate its Patient Transport Unit Next Generation (PTU NG) Intensive Care Unit into the rear of the aircraft or the Business Class suites. If necessary, it could also be built into the bed in the master suite, although the age of the principal passenger is a factor here.

Given the extreme range of the aircraft (7,285nm in airline trim) and the low passenger count, several Humidifier Onboard systems from CTT Systems will be installed throughout the cabin to raise comfort levels, as well as in the cockpit and crew rest compartments. Additionally, the Swedish company's dehumidifiers will be installed in the crown to prevent condensation soaking into the insulation blankets and adding unnecessary weight.

Timm said the VVIP Boeing BBJ 777-9 concept closely follows that of the 747s, although actual configurations are confidential.

Boeing BBJ 777-9

Wingspan (m)	71.8
Height (m)	19.5
Length (m)	76.7
Max. Take-off Weight (lbs)	775,000
Max. Landing Weight (lbs)	587,000
Max. Zero Fuel (lbs)	562,000
Interior Allowance (lbs)	65,000
Cabin (sq ft)	3,689
Cargo Volume (cu ft)	7,707
Fuel Capacity (US Gallons)	52,136
Range NM (75 passengers)	11,025

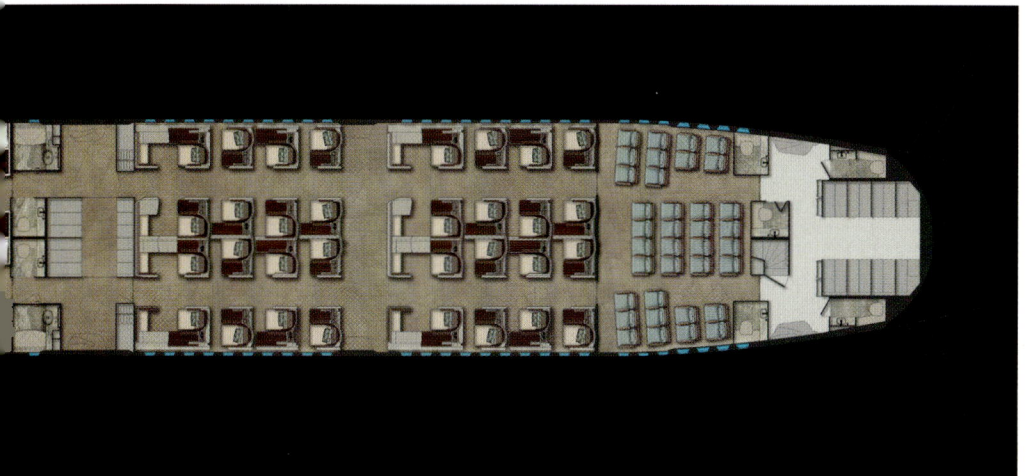

KLM TRANSFORMATION

KLM's
TRIPLE-SEVEN
TRANSFORMATION

Gordon Smith joins a special flight to Cape Town to meet some of the key players behind the project to overhaul the Dutch flag carrier's widebody workhorse

At the summer 2023 Paris Air Show, the presence of the Boeing 777X – complete with its novel folding wingtips – emerged as one of Le Bourget's most popular attractions. As Boeing executives will happily attest, the next-generation widebody has an impressive roll-call of future operators eager to leverage its improved performance and specifications; when the type finally enters revenue service, that is.

While all eyes are on the much-delayed 777X programme, many existing customers of the original 777 platform are making wholesale improvements to their more mature -200 and -300 fleets. The latest carrier to take on the task is KLM, which is giving its mid-life models a major facelift. Acknowledging that the Amsterdam/Schiphol-based airline was starting to lag behind big-name rivals and even its own joint-venture partners, the result is a significant improvement to the cabins of its long-haul flagship from front to back.

Radical refresh

KLM chiefs have unveiled not one, but two fresh cabin concepts in 2023. The previous year saw the debut of Premium Comfort on the 787 Dreamliner, a brand-new product and KLM's upper mid-market answer to premium economy, designed in partnership with Collins Aerospace (see *Airliner World*, November 2022). Now, attention turns to the 777s, with a huge overhaul of its 31-strong fleet.

After more than three years of development, the new business class cabin was formally introduced to the flying public on board Flight KL597 on June 28 between Amsterdam and Cape Town. Ahead of departure to South Africa, *Airliner World* caught up with Jacob Post, KLM's design lead for the programme, who offered valuable insight into the project. "As part of our extensive research, we invited several seat suppliers to our head office along with 21 'ultimate' frequent flyers. We tested the seats with them for several hours and alongside interviews, we observed how our passengers worked, ate and relaxed in the various products. These findings helped us select the best overall option," revealed Post, who has been with the airline since 2011 and honed his skills at the Delft University of Technology in the Netherlands.

The winning seat is the Jamco Venture – a platform that is likely to be familiar with KLM's regular customers. An earlier model is already found on the company's 787-10 Dreamliner, and until now has been considered KLM's best business class seat. But don't be fooled – bringing the Venture to the new-look 777 was more than a simple copy and paste job. Post and his ambitious colleagues, working closely with Jamco, wanted to take things a step further. The team agreed there wasn't a need to radically change the core product (which is popular for its relatively generous proportions), but acknowledged there were still improvements to make.

Unusually for a project of this scale, KLM kept most of the design effort in-house, with Post calling

BELOW • *KLM has embarked on an ambitious programme that will see it overhaul the cabins of its 31-strong Boeing 777 fleet.*
AIRTEAMIMAGES.COM/ MATTHIEU DOUHAIRE

ABOVE • *KLM's new Boeing 777 cabin concept was the second unveiled by the Dutch flag carrier in 2023 after the Premium Comfort offering rolled out on its 787 Dreamliners.* KLM

LEFT • *The Amsterdam-based flag carrier expects to keep its 777-300ERs well into the next decade, though the older -200 series is due to be phased out from 2028.* AIRTEAMIMAGES.COM/ VINCENZO PACE

on Dutch designer Arian Brekveld when he needed a fresh pair of eyes. KLM aficionados may recognise the latter's name from previous company installations; he was part of the recent Premium Comfort project and helped give the 747-400 its final cabin overhaul before the jumbo was retired.

Industry innovation

World Business Class has been KLM's most prestigious cabin since 1993, when the airline phased out its top-tier First Class offering. The decision initially raised eyebrows, but it's now widely seen as a shrewd move and one that many rivals have followed.

In total, 14 modifications have been made to the Venture variant found on the -10 Dreamliner, ranging from subtle tweaks to more substantial additions. The most obvious of these is the sliding door, bringing KLM in line with the international benchmark for long-haul premium flying.

Although the primary concept is nothing new, the way it's been incorporated by KLM and Jamco is innovative and unlike anything else currently in revenue service. Notably, it is made of an artificial leather-like material and is surprisingly flexible. It's also reassuringly easy to operate, using a magnetic-based system instead of mechanical locks found on earlier examples at other carriers. Indeed, these first-generation doors can weigh up to 15-20kg; by contrast, KLM's new approach comes in at just 8kg – a sizeable saving that feeds into the company's wider focus on sustainability.

The efficiencies extend beyond the door itself, as Post explained: "The seat is also very lightweight as the full mechanism is based on just one motor. When you consider that each motor is around 10kg and some seats can have up to three, we're saving 20kg at every seat." The cabin overhaul also heralds the end of the 2-2-2 configuration in business, bringing direct-aisle access to the fleet for the first time.

Speaking to *Airliner World* on board PH-BVA (c/n 35671), the first 777-300ER with the new cabin, was Olaf Stokman, KLM's director of customer experience. He said a balance between privacy and openness had been found and described the result as a "game-changer" for the airline: "We're trying to keep things elegant; it isn't a heavy blocking door that takes all the service interaction away. The crew are telling us that even when it is closed, there are still opportunities to interact with passengers." He added that this quest for elegance extends to the use of softer materials and less use of plastic and metallic surfaces, in line with passenger feedback on previous iterations.

A tall task

With each of KLM's 777-200 and -300s having 35 business class seats, and a total of 31 aircraft to retrofit, it's a big job, and that's before changes further back on the aircraft are considered. The carrier is also using the downtime to install its new Premium Comfort cabin across the 777 fleet – until now the exclusive preserve of its Dreamliners. There are also more modest improvements in economy, where updated seat cushions are being added.

Despite the scale of the task, Stokman confirmed that KLM is aiming to have all the jets kitted out with the new cabins in just 12 months, with the bulk of the work taking place locally through KLM's in-house MRO.

The job has been timed to coincide with the aircraft's midlife update, as many of the carrier's 777s are now more than a decade old. Like many legacy operators, KLM typically flies its long-haul jets for around 20-25 years before retirement, so the changes made today need to stand the test of time.

BELOW • *The cabin upgrades will be rolled out across both the Boeing 777-200ER and -300ER families.* AIRTEAMIMAGES.COM/DAAN VAN DER HEIJDEN

> With each of KLM's 777-200 and -300s having 35 business class seats, and a total of 31 aircraft to retrofit, it's a big job, and that's before changes further back in the aircraft are considered...

ABOVE LEFT • **KLM has selected the Jamco Venture seat for its new premium cabin.** KLM

ABOVE RIGHT • **The new premium cabin dispenses with the long-standing 2-2-2 layout in favour of direct-aisle access for all seats.** KLM

BELOW • **The Venture suite incorporates a sliding door alongside 13 other tweaks and changes including relocated power points and easy-access storage areas.** GORDON SMITH

BELOW INSET • **There's an array of options and settings to customise the seat.** GORDON SMITH

Company officials confirmed that the -300s are due to remain in the fleet well into the 2030s, while the smaller and more mature -200 variant is due to be phased out from 2028, based on current schedules. This will leave KLM's Airbus A330-200s and -300s as the last twin-aisle type without direct-aisle access in business class, though a senior source revealed the jets are due to be phased out "pretty soon", with all expected to be gone by 2028.

Acutely aware of the lead-in times between ordering new aircraft and seeing them delivered, Stokman confirmed that a widebody fleet replacement programme is "very much on the table", with the usual suspects in contention: "In the next six months we'll have a decision on a replacement for the A330, and there are many factors to consider. For example, we understand that the 777Xs would come pretty late [if ordered] in 2029, but then there are other options; we could look at more 787-10s, and of course the A350-900 and -1000. They're all being studied."

Reflecting on the progress made, but also the challenges ahead, KLM's EVP customer experience, Boet Kreiken, admitted that the 777 upgrade programme has been particularly ambitious, but that the risks have paid rewards: "We always tender and we always check everything out, but we ultimately found the technology at Jamco and the way they work with us to be the best. This wasn't an easy project – to create this kind of door is very complex – but the Jamco team were eager and ready in their mindset to do it."

Kreiken acknowledged that COVID-19 and more recent industry-wide capacity issues had caused headaches, but struck a more optimistic note looking forward: "The pandemic set us back three or four years. Financially we had to survive and lower our costs, pay back all kinds of loans and reduce our capital spending to a minimum.

"The supply chain for this specific project has also been very challenging. We've had several delays, which put us back another two to three months, but these things are always a learning curve. Although our first aircraft took around 15-16 days to retrofit, we hope to reduce this to nearer 11 days by the time the project nears completion. I'm incredibly proud of what we've delivered. It really is the result of a world-class team."

More than a door

KLM's first sliding door has grabbed the headlines, but there are 13 other improvements that have been made to the earlier model, as KLM's Jacob Post explained: "I was at the Aircraft Interiors Exhibition (AIX) in Hamburg and looked at all the various different seats on offer. Some looked very nice, but you'd later discover that things weren't very handy, or perhaps that the armrests weren't comfortable. Often these aren't immediately obvious, but they can be hugely important."

Following customer comments and his own research, additions and improvements include a forward-facing in-seat power supply (no longer tucked awkwardly behind your ear) plus a wireless option, a recessed bottle holder, more secure easy-access storage and a broader range of options for adjusting the seat. Post explained that these changes and ten others have been rooted in the 'three Cs' philosophy, which gives passengers greater control, comfort and customisation.

THE DESTINATION FOR AVIATION ENTHUSIASTS

Visit us today and discover all our publications

Aviation News is renowned for providing the best coverage of every branch of aviation.

Airforces Monthly is devoted to modern military aircraft and their air arms.

SIMPLY SCAN THE **QR CODE** OF YOUR FAVOURITE TITLE ABOVE TO FIND OUT MORE!

FREE P&P* when you order

shop.keypublishing.com

Call +44 (0)1780 480404 *(Mon to Fri 9am - 5.30pm GMT)*

714/24

SUBSCRIBE TODAY!

Air International has established an unrivalled reputation for authoritative reporting across the full spectrum of aviation subjects.

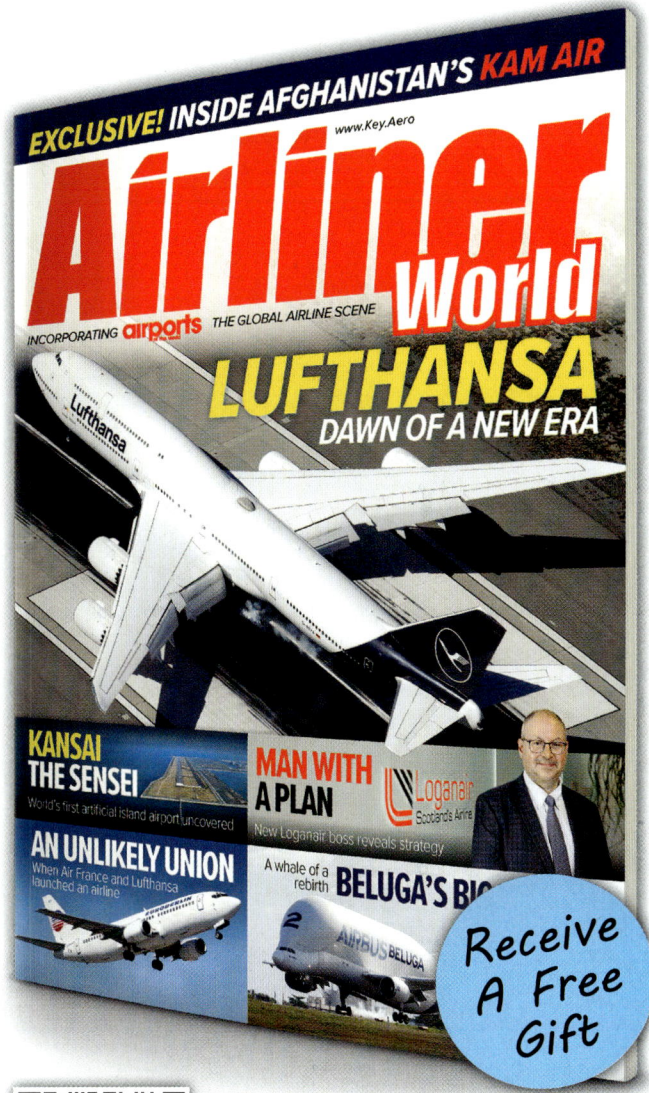

Airliner World magazine is the biggest-selling commercial aviation magazine in the world and is a must-read for anyone interested, in or associated with, the global airline scene.

from our online shop...
/collections/subscriptions

*Free 2nd class P&P on all UK & BFPO orders. Overseas charges apply.

Boeing's 777X

Mark Broadbent outlines Boeing's new 777X variants.

Four years after its formal launch in November 2013, the Boeing 777X programme was gathering pace. Basic engineering was approaching completion, the supply chain was gearing up, qualification testing was in progress and building work on the first aircraft iwa under way.

At the time, Terry Beezhold, 777X vice-president and chief project engineer, told the author: "This is an exciting phase. After several years developing and reducing risk for the flight test programme now we're in the build phase."

Boeing is developing two new Triple Sevens in the 777X programme, the 777-9 and 777-8. The company hopes these aircraft will continue the popularity well into the future of what has been the most successful widebody twin-jet airliner ever built. By spring 2024, over 2,200 Triple Sevens had been sold, with more than 1,700 of those delivered.

The 777-9 is being developed first.

Largest Twin-Jet

Size will make the 777-9 stand out. The aircraft will be 251ft 9in in length, making it 7ft longer than the 777-300ER; four extra fuselage frames give it the extra length compared to the current-production model.

It will be the longest airliner ever built by Boeing, slightly longer

ABOVE • *The two Boeing 777X versions have attracted 481 orders to date.* BOEING

than the 250ft 2in-long 747-8 and 13ft 2in longer than the Airbus A380 at 238ft 7in in length. Such is the new Triple Seven's length that it will be only 23ft 10in shorter than the sole Antonov An-225 Myria, the world's largest aircraft, which is 275ft 7in long. In flight the 777-9's wingspan will be 235ft 5in – not as wide as the A380's 261ft 8in reach and some way down on the An-225's huge 290ft, but wider than the 777-300ER's 212ft 9in.

The 777-9 is the first twin-engine airliner designed to carry more than 400 passengers. According to Boeing's latest provisional Aircraft Characteristics for Airport Planning document, the jet will have capacity for 414 seats in a standard two-class seat layout, up from the 777-300ER's 396 two-class. Scalloped frames, which have widened the cabin by two inches on either side of the fuselage compared to the 777-300ER, will allow for ten-abreast seating in a typical 3-4-3 seat layout.

For the major network airlines that form the customer base for widebody aircraft, the 777-9's greater seat capacity provides the potential to carry more of

BELOW • *The primary feature of Boeing's 777-8 is the aircraft's range.*
BOEING

> "Boeing's opinion is that there's no other aircraft in the part of the market where the 777-9 sits and said the company sees the A350-1000 as: "actually a more direct competitor to the 777-8, although our view is that we have a much more capable airplane in the 777-8." Terry Beezhold, Boeing's 777X vice-president and chief project engineer

Compared to the 777-300ER, the 777-9 has the following notable differences

- Overall length is 9ft 4in longer
- Folded wingspan is the same, unfolded wingspan is 22ft 9in wider
- Horizontal stabiliser is 9ft 10in wider
- Wheelbase is 3ft 7in longer
- Engine to fuselage centreline is 3ft 3in further outboard
- Vertical tail maximum height is < 3ft higher
- Main landing gear width is 6in narrower

Data: Boeing

the travellers they prize the most: those flying in lucrative premium classes.

There's more revenue-raising potential compared to earlier 777s, thanks to greater lower-deck cargo volume. With an 8,131ft3 lower-deck cargo hold, compared to 7,120ft3 on the 777-300ER, the 777-9 will be able to carry 48 LD-3s (26 in the forward hold and 22 in the rear hold) if the optional rear cargo door is selected, up from 44 LD-3s on the 777-300ER.

According to Aircraft Characteristics for Airport Planning, the 777-9's basic maximum take-off weight (MTOW) will be 775,000lb, the same as the 777-300ER.

All these statistics and performance figures look set to cement the 777's position as the largest twin-jet airliner: it truly will be a big twin.

Range and Efficiencies

At 251ft 9in long the second new 777X variant, the 777-8, will be nearly 23ft shorter than the 777-9. It will have fewer seats than its sister aircraft (365 passengers, two classes), and although the figures have yet to be disclosed, the shortened fuselage inevitably means less underfloor cargo capacity.

However, the 777-8's primary feature will be its range. It will be able to fly 8,745 nautical miles, which Boeing says opens new route development possibilities for airlines. Range maps for the variant show the aircraft will be capable of flying ultra-long-haul city pairs such as London Heathrow–Perth and New York JFK–Auckland non-stop, assuming a 395-passenger, two-class layout.

As with previous widebody aircraft families, including the older Triple Seven variants, the 777-9 and 777-8 are designed to be complementary. Beezhold said: "The 777-9 gives you large capacity and then the 777-8 gives you range. [The 777X has] got the range if you need range, or if you don't it has tremendous flexibility in terms of high-altitude airports and hot-weather performance."

Boeing says both 777X variants will be able to fly hot and high sectors (for example, Madrid–Mexico City), long and hot (such as Los Angeles–Dubai), long and high-payload (such as Sydney–Sao Paulo) and ultra-long haul (for instance, New York JFK–Singapore).

It should be added here that although the 777-9 is not optimised for ultra-long range like the 777-8, it will hardly be short legged; its 7,525 nautical miles capability means it will be able to fly London–Los Angeles or New York JFK–Hong Kong, assuming a 426-passenger, two-class layout and a 351,530lb MTOW.

The 777Xs will bring performance improvements on earlier Triple Sevens. The 777-9's capacity and range is an increase from the 777-300ER's 396 seats and two classes and 7,370 nautical miles range. The 777-8's capabilities are up from 317 seats and 8,555 nautical miles range of the current-production 777-200LR, previously the longest-range 777.

In efficiency terms, Boeing claims the 777X variants will be 20% more fuel efficient per seat than the 777-300ER. The company claims that compared to the Airbus A350-1000 - the principal competition in the high-capacity long-range market for twin-jet airliners - the 777Xs will be 12% more fuel efficient per seat and 10% cheaper to operate and generate 12% less carbon dioxide emissions.

Beezhold said Boeing's opinion is that there's no other aircraft in the part of the market where the 777-9 sits and said the company sees the A350-1000 as: "actually a more direct competitor to the 777-8, although our view is that we have a much more capable airplane in the 777-8."

Integration and Reliability Testing

Boeing regards maturity testing as especially important for the 777X. This is perhaps unsurprising, given the bad publicity caused by the development delays that afflicted its last new widebody airliner, the 787. Although later events would lead to further delays with the aircraft, one 2020 comment from Terry

Key Facts: 777X

- At 251ft 9in in length, the 777-9 is the longest airliner Boeing has ever built and 7ft longer than the 777-300ER
- Its GE9X engines have a 134in fan diameter, the largest fan diameter developed to date for any jet engine
- The 777-9 is the first twin-engine airliner designed to carry more than 400 passengers
- Folding wingtips extend and retract to ensure ICAO Code E compatibility
- Commonality in systems with the 787 Dreamliner and current-production 777s
- Touchscreens in the flight deck

Data: Boeing

Boeing 777X Orders and Commitments		
Airline	777-8	777-9
ANA Holdings		20
British Airways		18
Cathay Pacific Airways		21
Emirates	35	170
Etihad Airways	8	17
Air India		10
Lufthansa		27
Qatar Airways	24	50
Singapore Airlines		31
Unidentified		10
Total	67	374

Source: Boeing Orders and Deliveries Correct to spring 2024. NB. Not including 777-F orders

ABOVE • *Boeing 777-9 made the type's first flight from Everett-Paine Field Washington on January 25, 2020.* BOEING

Beezhold to the author indicated the experience has left its mark on the company. He said: "One of the things we've done on this programme is to drive maturity into all of the systems much earlier than what we've done historically which was to drive all the qualification testing to completion much earlier."

During the second half of 2018, Boeing completed qualification testing. Beezhold said: "That means we completed the full hardware and full environmental aspects/conditions, all the systems testing, all the EMI [electronic magnetic interference] testing. We do that across all of our suppliers so they're all responsible both to design and to qualification testing of their equipment.

"We've also asked our suppliers, especially on new equipment, to do something we call reliability enhancement testing. They built their initial prototype of the hardware and then put it through a preliminary qualification test and tested it above the vibration levels to look for the weak link of the hardware. Then they made design changes to make it more robust so it can withstand higher levels than what we'd normally qualify."

Beezhold said the process is designed to build a high level of reliability and robustness into the 777X's design which, in his words, "ultimately then goes to qualification testing, usually with ease, and 'hardens' the design before full testing. We've done that so we do not catch issues at an aircraft level during the flight test programme. That dramatically reduces the risk of having to make changes late in the programme and provide a mature aircraft during flight test."

For the major network airlines that form the customer base for widebody aircraft, the 777-9's greater seat capacity provides the potential to carry more of the travellers they prize the most: those flying in lucrative premium classes.

Boeing 777-8

Boeing 777-8 Characteristics

Wingspan (tips extended)	235ft 5in
Wingspan (tips folded)	212ft 9in
Wing area	5,025ft^2
Length	232ft 6in
Height	63ft 11in
Max design taxi weight	777,000lb
Max take-off weight	775,000lb
Max landing weight	To be disclosed
Max zero fuel weight	TBD
Operating empty weight	TBD
Max structural payload	TBD
Total cargo volume	TBD
Lower deck cargo volume	8,131ft^3
Lower deck cargo	TBD
Useable fuel	TBD
Cruise speed	Mach 0.85
Ceiling	TBD
Seating	395 passengers two-class
Range	8,745 nautical miles
Engines	Two General Electric GE9Xs, each generating 100,000lb of thrust

Source: Boeing
With the flight test programme ongoing, some figures have yet to be confirmed.

BOEING

Boeing 777-9

Boeing 777-9 Characteristics

Wingspan (tips extended)	235ft 5in
Wingspan (tips folded)	212ft 8in
Wing area	5,025ft^2
Length	251ft 9in
Height	64ft 1in
Max design taxi weight	777,000lb
Max design take-off weight	775,000lb
Max design landing weight	587,000lb
Max design zero fuel weight	562,000lb
Operating empty weight	TBD
Max structural payload	TBD
Lower deck cargo volume	8,131ft^3
Lower deck cargo	46 LD-3 containers (26 forward, 20 aft) as standard, or 48 LD-3 containers (26 forward, 22 aft) with large aft cargo door option
Usable fuel	52,300 US gal
Cruise speed	Mach 0.85
Ceiling	TBD
Seating	426 passengers two-class or 349 three-class
Range	7,285 nautical miles
Engines	Two General Electric GE9Xs, each generating 100,000lb of thrust

Source: Boeing Characteristics for Airport Planning

Wing

Mark Broadbent details the design and aerodynamics of the 777X wing.

The 777X's GE Aviation GE9X turbofan engines are the largest commercial aero engines ever built. They will play a major part in the new Triple Sevens achieving their promised performance. However, the engines are only part of the equation. The 777X's wings have a major role, too.

The variants' wings feature extensive use of carbon fibre reinforced plastic composites, with the panels, skins, stringers, and the entire spar all made from the material. At 105ft long, the spar is the largest single-piece composite part ever developed for an airliner.

As with any composite materials in an airframe, the composite wing is designed to eliminate the typical features of a traditional metallic structure, such as fasteners, joints, and overlaps, which creates a weight saving and a performance benefit. The composite panels, skins, stringers and spar are produced at Boeing's Everett factory, the home of the 777, in the new Composite Wing Centre adjacent to the 777's final assembly line. The Boeing Fabrication facility in St Louis, Missouri, produces other composite wing components, including the leading and trailing edges.

RIGHT • *A key visual difference from earlier 777 models, is something never seen before on a commercial airliner: folding wingtips.*
ALL IMAGES BOEING

www.key.aero 81

Folding Mechanism

Another important feature of the 777X variants' wings, which will also provide a key visual difference from earlier models, is something never seen before on a commercial airliner: folding wingtips. Boeing wanted a wide wingspan for the 777X, as per the company's overall approach to widebody aircraft wing design, which is to maximise aspect ratio to create superior lift-to-drag characteristics.

Wide wingspans impose limitations, however. International Civil Aviation Organization regulations governing safety separations between aircraft and ground objects at airports for taxiway and gate compatibility classify aircraft into different design codes. Aircraft with wingspans greater than 170ft 7in but less than 213ft 2in are classified in Code E and aircraft with wingspans between 213ft 2in and 262ft 4in, such as the 747-8 and A380, are categorised separately as Code F.

The full 235ft 5in wingspan would put the 777Xs into Code F rather than Code E, where the current-production models sit with their 212ft 9in wingspans. The new variants would therefore be precluded from using the same gates, as today's jets and airports would potentially be required to make infrastructure changes to accept 777Xs.

Boeing's solution? Seven-foot long wingtips that fold upwards and downwards. On the ground, with these outboard sections in an upright position, the 777X will have the same 212ft 9in wingspan as the current models to maintain Code E compatibility. Using a dedicated control panel on the flight deck the crew will be able to unfold the tips prior to departure to the full span for flight.

Boeing's chief project engineer Terry Beezhold said: "When we were looking at the wing design, where the optimum span would be to provide the highest efficiency, we did look at putting winglets on, but the right answer was to go with this longer span wing and then put on the folding wingtip to maintain airport compatibility. We wanted to maintain Code E classification."

ABOVE AND RIGHT • *The wing tip partly unfolded.* BOEING

BELOW • *An interesting view of the wing's lead edge on the 777X.* BOEING

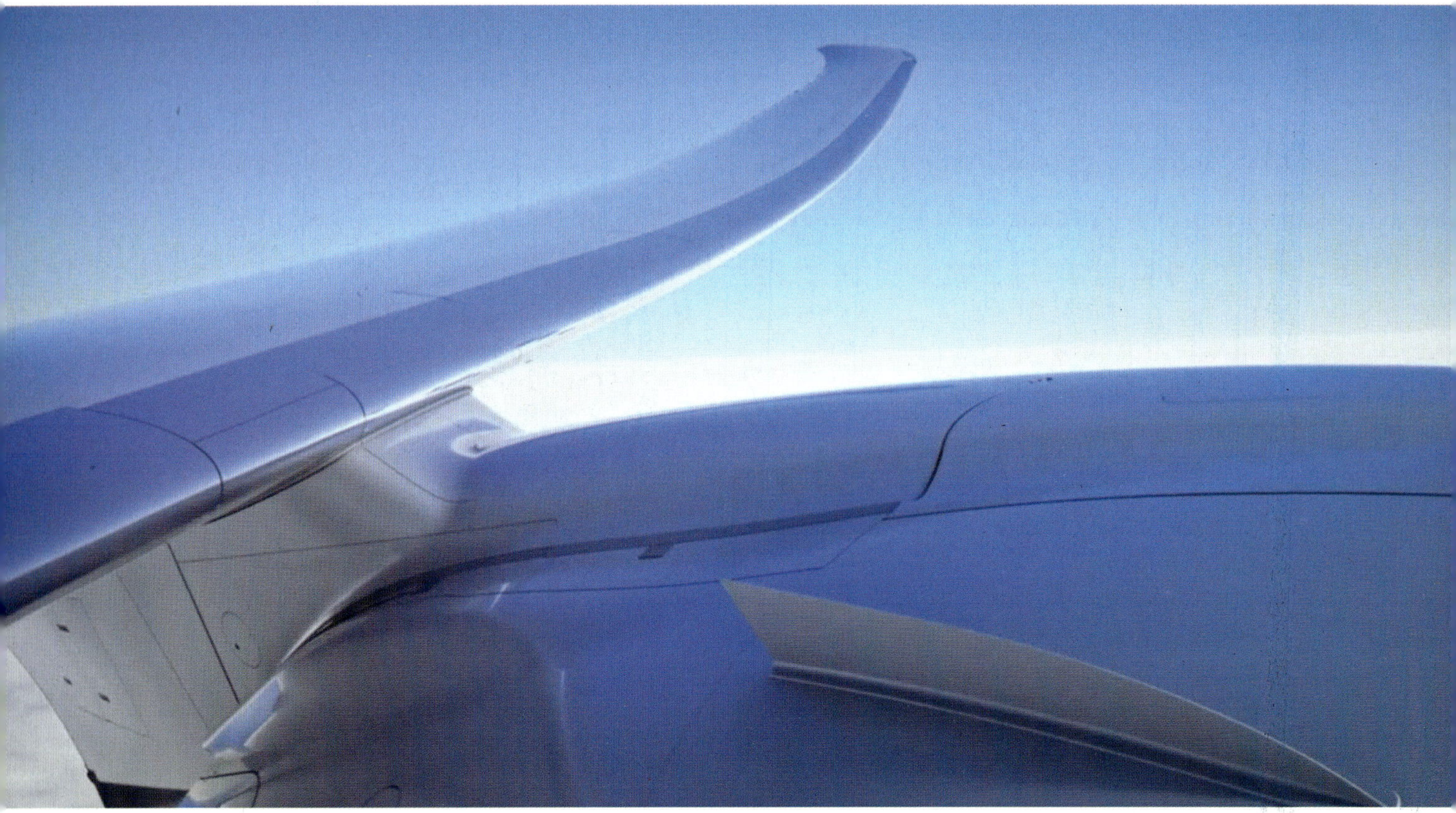

> *Although the 777X flight deck will have the familiar Rockwell Collins multifunction displays, interfaces, checklists, and dual head-up displays, one big difference with older 777s is the five large-format LCD screens, as opposed to the current generation's six smaller screens.*

position. The entire subsystem is self-contained in the wing loft area.

German company Liebherr Aerospace is supplying the wing fold, drawing from its experience designing hydraulic actuation systems for primary flight controls. The fold mechanism will be integrated into the wingtip assembly by Boeing at the St Louis factory, which is fabricating the wingtip as part of its 777X work package.

The composite wing and its folding tips are not the only airframe differences between the 777X variants and earlier models. To optimise for drag and ensure there are no steps and gaps in the structure that create inefficiencies, there are completely redesigned fuselage fairings, a new wing-to-fuselage fairing, and a new empennage.

is integrated into the wing to really maximise the total efficiency, versus having to make compromises for different engine types."

Aerodynamic Efficiencies

Another influence on wing efficiency is loading. Aircraft manufacturers have become increasingly interested in designing ways to optimise wing profile in flight to account for changing loads.

On the 777X there is a variable camber trailing edge and a vertical gust suppression system. Variable camber adapts the position of the wing and the gust suppression system deploys the flaps, ailerons, and spoilers to move the loading of gusts around the wing to give a more aerodynamically efficient wing shape.

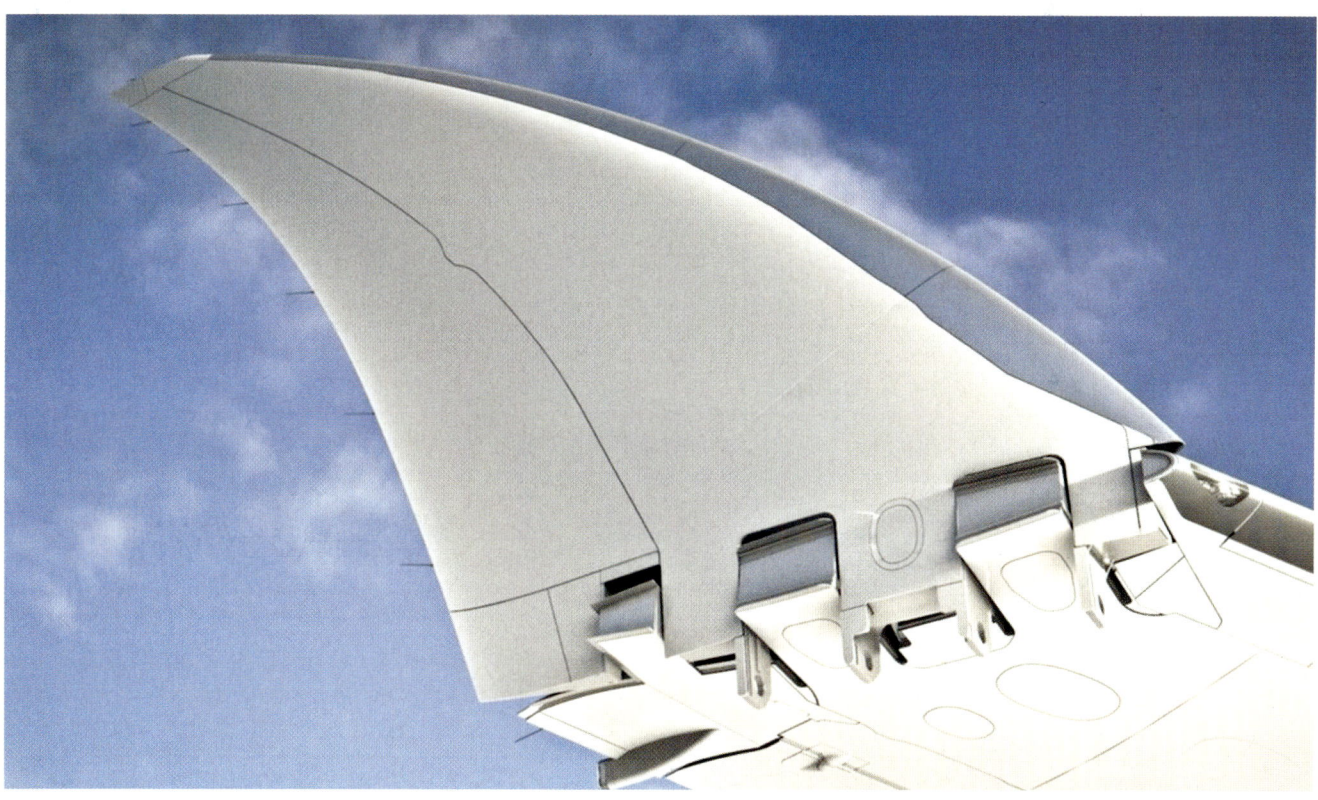

Beezhold said reliability was key to the folding wingtip's viability. He insisted: "We have come up with a very simple yet robust mechanism to control the wing fold." The system works, he explained, through mechanical actuation. Redundancy from the 777X's integrated drive train is used to power a motor. This motor drives a rotating actuator that raises and lowers the wingtips when commanded by the flight deck control panel. Pins lock the tips when they are raised and lowered to the desired

Beezhold also highlighted the GE9X engine nacelles as an important aerodynamic achievement. Although GE designs the powerplant, Boeing is responsible for the nacelle, the thrust reverser, and the inlet. Beezhold said natural laminar flow was used to ensure optimal efficiency for these parts.

He added having a single-source engine supplier in the form of GE was beneficial: "You can have multiple engine offerings, but we partnered GE so we could go in with them and optimise the way that engine

Beezhold explained these systems work because accelerometers mounted on the wing measure vertical and lateral separation of the gusts over the wing. These sensors automatically send electronic signals to the actuators, which then make tiny adjustments to the flight controls to distribute the loading evenly across the wing to ensure optimal airflow and minimal drag.

The combination of the wingspan and the various aerodynamic efficiencies all working together

WING

"When we were looking at the wing design, where the optimum span would be to provide the highest efficiency, we did look at putting winglets on, but the right answer was to go with this longer span wing and then put on the folding wingtip to maintain airport compatibility. We wanted to maintain Code E classification." Terry Beezhold, Boeing's 777X vice-president and chief project engineer

ABOVE • *This computer generated image shows the 777X's wing profile in flight.* BOEING

BELOW • *A scale model of a 777-9 in the wind tunnel during early aerodynamic testing. Note the upward profile of the wing to replicate in flight aerodynamics.* BOEING

gives, Beezhold said, "the highest lift over drag efficiency aircraft ever developed".

Link to the 787

The 777X's use of composites in the wing and of variable camber and gust suppression technologies highlights a link between the 787 and the new Triple Sevens, but the crossover between the families goes much further.

Control laws from the Dreamliner's flight control system (FCS), including angle of bank protection and an automatic roll and yaw asymmetry compensation system that applies rudder if an engine is lost, have been integrated into the 777X FCS.

Beezhold continued: "For the 777X we've adapted the 787 Common Core System [CCS] to provide a much more advanced and capable platform for hosted functions that share a common set of computing resources."

The CCS is effectively the central nervous system of the aircraft, hosting avionics and utilities functions. On the current production 777s the CCS is a basic computing platform. The 777X's CCS, supplied by GE Aviation, is like the 787 CCS designed to eliminate the boxes and wiring that housed and supplied computing power aboard. GE Aviation says it provides a weight saving of hundreds of pounds on earlier 777s.

The 777X CCS is also designed to share common components with the 787 CCS. Its open system architecture means developers are only required to test and certify functions that have been altered and operators can scale the system depending on their needs; both are designed to minimise costs. Beezhold added: '[The 777X's CCS has] a lot more growth capability as we look ahead to the demands on systems like flight management where there's a huge amount of data."

Another similarity between the new Triple Sevens and the 787 is the flight deck. Boeing's CGIs show the 777X's flight deck will look much more like a 787's than a 777's. Like the Dreamliner, large-format LCD screens will be supplied by Rockwell Collins.

Hybrid Approach

Besides the link to the 787, there will also be extensive commonality with current-production Triple Sevens; a quite deliberate approach by Boeing. Beezhold acknowledged: "The 777 is very reliable, so one thing we wanted to ensure we did was to carry over the systems that are operating really well."

Among the key commonalities with the current models will be the fuselage barrels, which will be made from conventional aluminium like the current 777s, rather than composites like the Dreamliner's. Power for key systems such as the auxiliary power unit, hydraulics, wing anti-ice protection and cabin environment control systems will be drawn from a conventional pneumatic architecture using high-pressure bleed air diverted from the engines, rather than the electrical power architecture used on the 787.

The 777Xs' power generation system, supplied by UTC Aerospace, will comprise two 150kVA integrated drive generators, an auxiliary generator, three generator control units and a bus power control unit, which the company says will provide 25% more power than the system on current production 777s.

There will be lots that will be familiar to pilots, with those similar flight control laws mentioned earlier and Rockwell Collins avionics (used on current and legacy 777s). Boeing has also sought to position control switches in the same places. For instance, Beezhold said: "The overhead P5 panel is very similar to the 777 to minimise any kind of difference training. We wanted to make sure the crew interface [is] maintained to make sure that memory motion that flight crews have is unchanged."

All this commonality is by design to minimise key operational costs, such as spares management and pilot training. The intention is the new 777s will have a common type rating with all three 787 variants. This is not to say, however, that the 777-9 and 777-8 will not have their own novelties.

Although the flight deck will have the familiar Rockwell Collins multifunction displays, interfaces, checklists, and dual head-up displays, one big difference with older 777s is the five large-format LCD screens, as opposed to the current generation's six smaller screens. These displays will feature resistive technology that, by requiring a firm rather than a light touch to operate the display,

BELOW • *A flight test 777-9 on the Everett final assembly line during production work on the fuselage-wing join.*
BOEING

is designed to avoid unintentional interaction. The displays will also have bracing features for operation during turbulence and the lower display will be multitouch, meaning both pilots can simultaneously interact with the display.

When the design was announced, Rockwell Collins Commercial Systems' executive vice-president and chief operating officer Kent Statler said: "Touchscreens are everywhere in our lives. A touch-controlled flight deck environment makes it easier for pilots to manage information and do their jobs and speeds up the process to complete tasks."

From an operator's perspective, the flight deck is a good case study of the line Boeing has tried to walk with the 777X, taking the familiar and the proven and adding new elements. Beezhold summed up the approach: "The 777X is really a hybrid of the best of the [current] 777, the best of the 787 and some new technologies that don't feature on either of those models. It's about adapting to keep the commonality, but accounting for any differences."

COMPOSITE WING CENTRE

Boeing employees inspect the carbon fibre on a 777X prototype wing panel before curing at the Composite Wing Centre at Everett. BOEING

At 105ft long the Boeing 777X's spars are the largest single-piece carbon fibre reinforced plastic (CFRP) composite parts ever developed for an airliner. Along with the wing's panels, the spars are produced at the new Composite Wing Centre (CWC) that Boeing built specifically for the 777X at the Everett home of the Triple Seven.

The CWC produces four spars (front, rear, right and left) and four panels (upper, lower, right and left). Another factory, Boeing Fabrication in St Louis, Missouri, supplies the wing's leading and trailing edges, ribs, and folding tips.

Building Spars

Back in 2017, Kevin Bartelson, 777X wing fabrication leader, gave the author a detailed explanation of the work undertaken in the CWC, which covers 1.2 million ft2 in area. The build process for both the spars and panels begins in the clean room, where carbon fibre pre-preg tape (a reinforced pliable and uncured carbon fibre tape which has been pre-impregnated with a resin system) is laid down. Next, the parts are moved using automated guided vehicles (AGVs) to post-care for curing in the autoclave and subsequent trimming and inspection. The AGVs move components, work stands and robotic arms around the factory floor.

Bartelson first explained the build process for the spars. Two automated fibre placement machines are used to lay down the tape for the spars (one machine for the front spar, one for the rear). An automated gantry picks up the head of the machine and runs it back and forth along the length of the spar to lay down the carbon fibre. The gantry can drop the head of a machine, pick up another head and return to work within two minutes.

The head has 16 spindles on it and with each spindle laying down 0.5in of tape the machines lay down 8in of tape at a time. More than 100 layers of tape are required to build up each spar.

Bartelson said: "We lay the tape in various directions. We lay it down with zero-degree direction the length of the spar, a 90° direction and plus 45° and minus 45°. That gives it strength characteristics in all directions."

The automated fibre placement machines have been supplied by ElectroImpact. Bartelson said: "These are their newest generation of machines. The next aircraft programme will get the next generation, but right now we've got the fastest machines that do things other machines can't. We're laying a half-inch tape around a pretty complex contour; no one's ever done that before."

Autoclave

A layer of fibreglass is added to the spar before an AGV transports the tool with the spar on it through a cross-aisle in the building to the autoclave. A ramp will be lowered to enable the AGV to load the spar into the autoclave. The

Wing Factory

The 777X's wing, the largest composite part ever made for an aircraft, is produced in the Composite Wing Centre at Everett. **Mark Broadbent** reports on a facility which opened in 2017.

COMPOSITE WING CENTRE

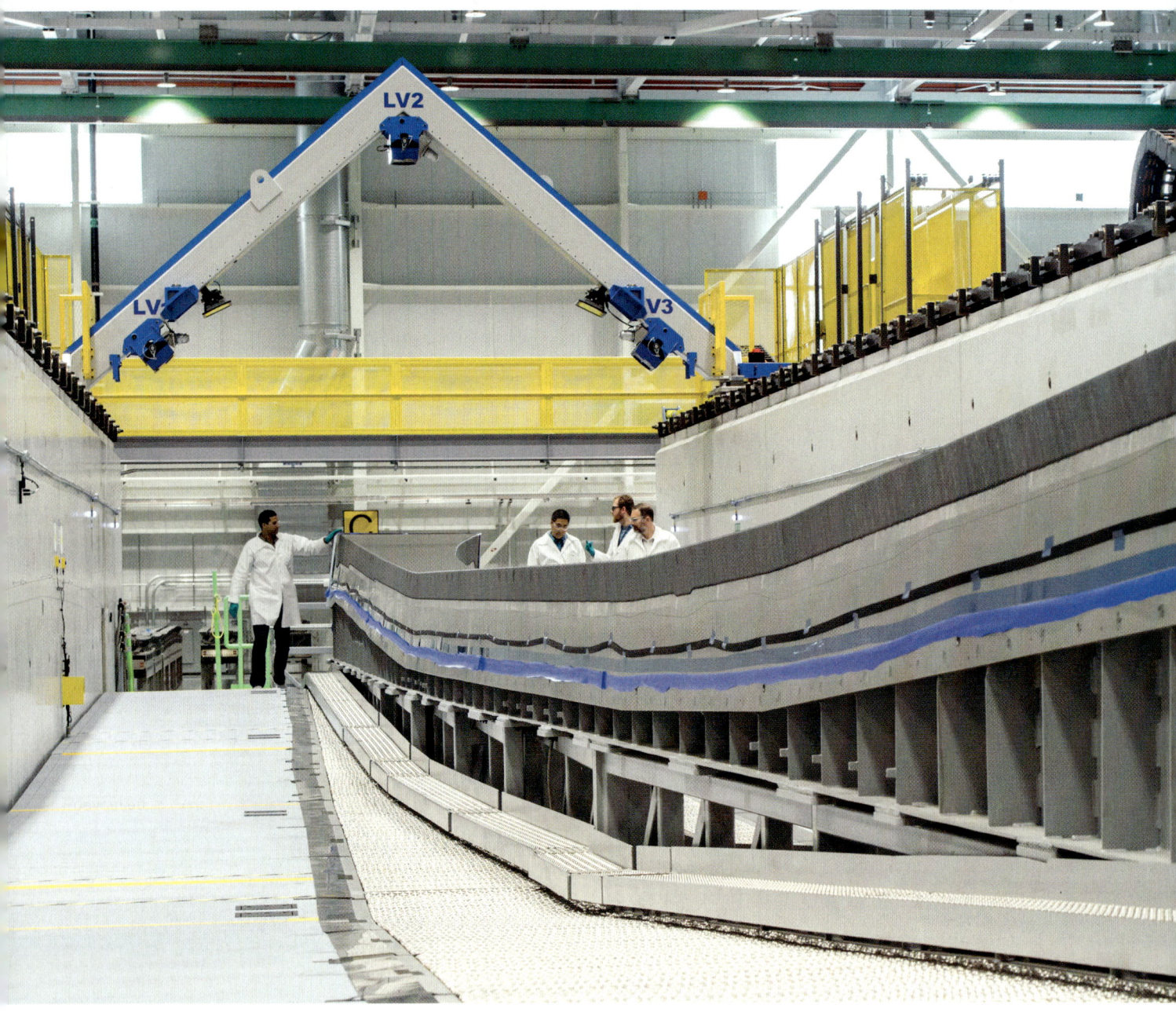

ABOVE • *The Composite Wing Centre in Everett produces four wing spars (front, rear, right, left), which at 105ft long are the largest composite parts ever produced for an airliner.* BOEING

AGV will then be withdrawn, the ramp lifted, the autoclave door closed and locked, allowing the cure cycle to begin.

Bartelson said: "Most cures are around 350°C and somewhere between four and ten hours long, depending on the parts you've got. They're always pressurised. When you pressurise, you're putting a vacuum bag on the part and pushing down with pressure, making sure you get all the air out and a solid laminate."

The systems required for pressurisation and nitrogen generation, and a need to minimise noise, means the autoclave is, in Bartelson's words, "a building within a building". The CWC will eventually have three autoclaves; each is 28ft in diameter and 120ft long – large enough to fit a 737 Classic fuselage inside it.

Post-cure, the autoclave doors will be opened, the ramp lowered and the AGV will go in and pick up the spar, bringing it out into the aisle. The vacuum bag will be removed, and the part taken out of the mould. Overhead cranes will take the spar for non-destructive inspection (NDI), where a robot will spray water at the part and send a signal through it to check whether there is a solid laminate.

The crane will then take the spar to a routing machine for trimming and drilling. After washing and a second NDI test to ensure there has been no delamination during the trimming and drilling, the spar will be painted.

Producing Panels

The four wing panels produced in the CWC have two basic pieces: the skin and stringers. Just like the spars these parts are prepared in the clean room, but the CFRP material for them is laid down in a separate part of the room to the spar, and it is laid down in a different way.

The skin is made by an automated fibre placement machine controlled by a gantry laying down more than 100 plies of 1.5in tape. Bartelson said: "It looks stiff but it's soft; literally, if you tried to pick up a corner of it, you'd ripple the whole thing."

Unlike the machine used to laminate the spars, which has spindles, the one used to lay down the tape for the skins has reels. Bartelson explained Boeing has found that a reel system works well for achieving the gradual contours a wing panel needs, while spindles are better for achieving the radical contours of a spar's u-shape.

The stringers provide stiffness along the length of the panel and are made by putting together an L shape, two L charges and what is termed a noodle to fill the triangular gap created when those three other parts are put together. A base charge is laid out flat on top of this assembly, which is sent to the autoclave

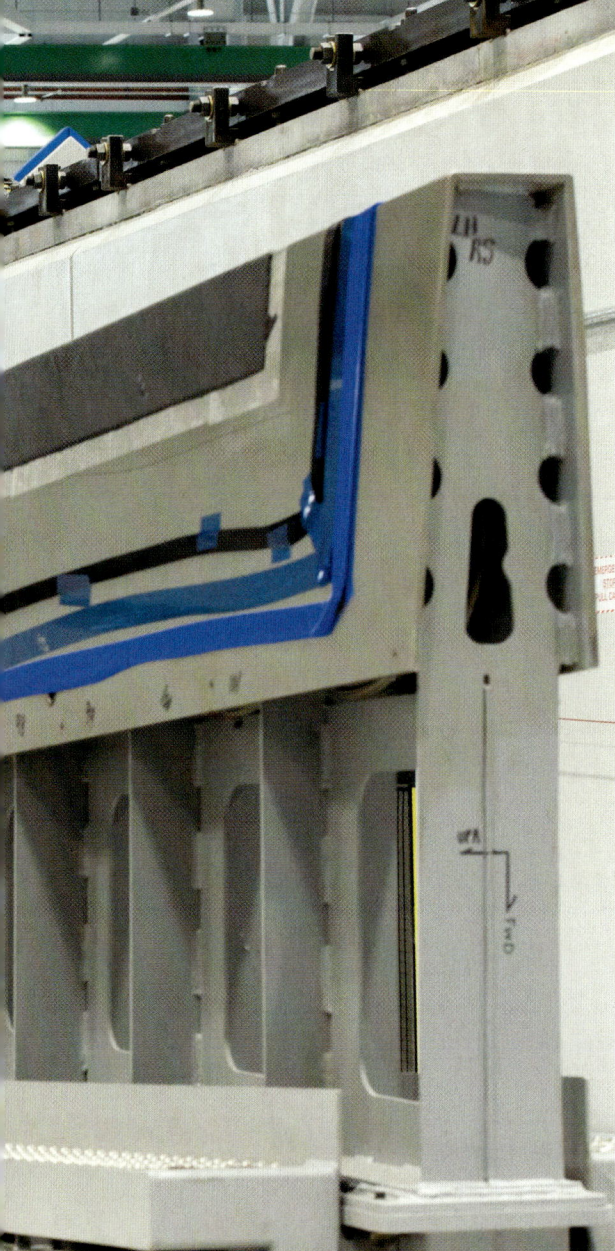

> "We lay the tape in various directions. We lay it down with zero-degree direction the length of the spar, a 90° direction and plus 45° and minus 45°. That gives it strength characteristics in all directions." Kevin Bartelson, 777X wing fabrication leader.

for curing. The 777X's wing has 66 stringers, divided between the four panels (23, 23, ten and ten respectively). Each stringer is 108ft long.

The term charge used above refers to composite charges, which is the use of nanoparticles to enhance strength. This is a process that involves binding two components together with each component holding an opposite charge.

After the stringers are formed, they will be sent directly to the autoclave. Two lifting fixtures called Overhead Machine Equipment (OHME) will be responsible for moving, lifting, and rotating the stringers; one fixture is used for ten of the 66 stringer configurations and the other fixture for the other 56 configurations.

Bartelson explained: "An overhead crane will come along and pick [the OHME] up and take it over to where we've built a stringer. It'll drop down and pneumatically pick the stringer up. That's why it has the rotating feature, to set [the stringer] down in another location. It's a way of turning the stringer to work on either side of it. The system can both lift and rotate, so the stringer will not twist."

After curing, the stringers will be trimmed, and NDI checked before being applied to the as yet uncured skin. The wing panel assembly with the soft, uncured skin and the hard, baked stringers attached will next go to the autoclave where the hard stringers will bond to the uncured skin to create the completed panel. This process is called co-bonding.

Post-cure, the finished panel will be demoulded. A crane will lift the panel and rotate it to a vertical position for an NDI test. It will be trimmed, inspected again, and drilled before it is washed, painted, and has brackets and clips installed.

Assembly

When the work on the panels is complete in the CWC, the panels will be sent directly across the Everett site to the main 777 final assembly building. When the spars have been fabricated, however, they will be moved to a separate facility, Building 4002, for subassembly work.

Holes will be drilled into them and fasteners, stiffeners and rib posts installed. Much of this work will be automated using machines supplied by the Spanish company MTorres,

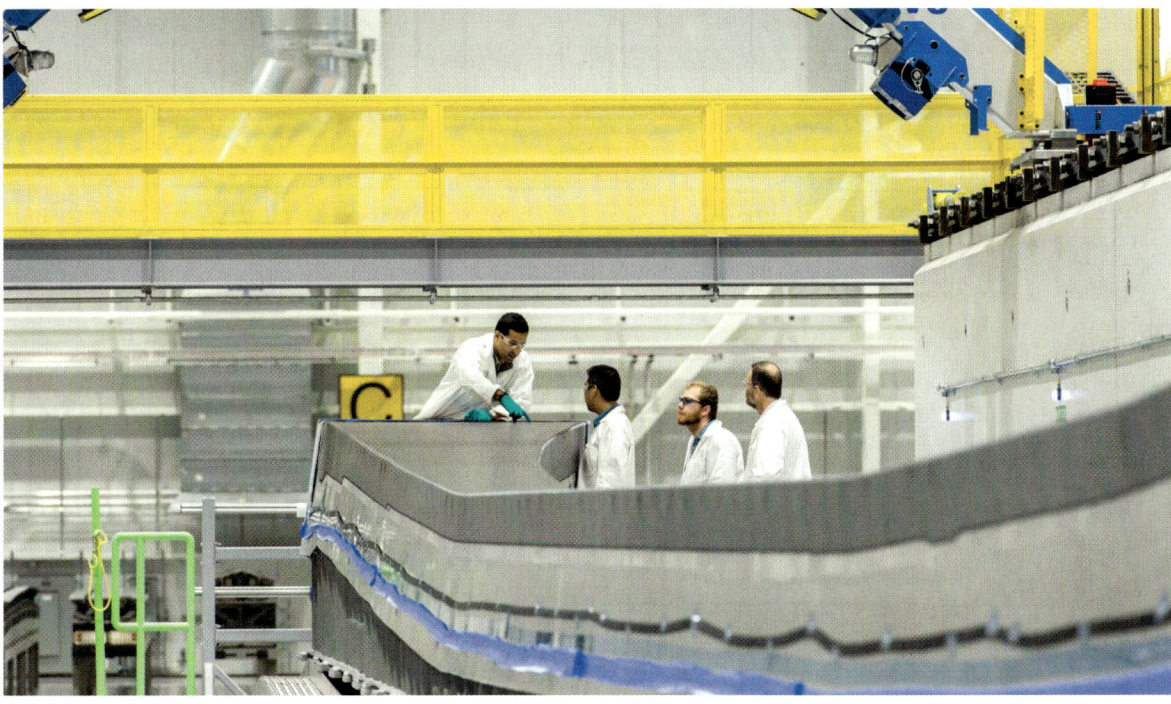

RIGHT • *Post-cure, the 777X's wing spars undergo non-destructive inspection before trimming and drilling. Here Boeing employees inspect a wing spar for the 777X static test aircraft.*
BOEING

COMPOSITE WING CENTRE

but more complex subassembly activities such as installing pinions will be done manually.

After this work is completed, the spars will be moved to the main final assembly building where they join the panels from the CWC and the leading and trailing edges, ribs, and folding tips, which will have arrived from St Louis. Wing assembly will then begin.

Bartelson explained there will be a change in the wing assembly process on the 777X: "Traditionally, we'd take two spars, attach the ribs to them and you get this funny-looking ladder; the ribs look like steps. Typically, we do that in a vertical position."

On the 777X, however, the spars and ribs will be joined on a horizontal build line. Following drilling, fastening, and sealing of the spars/ribs assembly, the upper and lower panels will be installed, which will be followed by further drilling, fastening, and sealing. Leading-edge and trailing-edge panel installation and in-tank work will follow before the wing-to-fuselage body join. The folding wingtips will be attached later.

Automation

With the laminating machines, the AGVs and the OHMEs there's an impressive extent of automation in the CWC. Bartelson said this helps efficiency and ergonomics: "When you lay down this type of material by hand you've got to use cloth to form it to the product. There's 100-plus layers of tape on the spar; can you imagine 100-plus layers of cloth that you've got to cut out? What we're doing here is using the machines for what they do well and our people for what they do well."

Automation also helps safety. Highlighting the fibre placement machine in spar build, Bartelson said the machine will not pass over any people on the factory floor. When it is dropping or picking up a head it passes over to an area where there are two cradles. He said: "It can drop its head in one of those slots and then the machine can go pick up another head or go park. Then this robot picks up the head out of that interactive area and presents it and it shuts down completely. It's a little feature we're pleased with; we've got to keep our people safe."

Practice Work

In 2016, Bartelson said, the focus with the CWC was completing building work on the facility and installing equipment. The following 12 months was about building practice parts, as part of the wider focus in the 777X programme to build maturity.

Practice spars, skins and stringers were produced, with the parts then cut up and analysed to verify the components being produced by the CWC were as expected; at the time of this interview originally conducted for AIR International magazine, for example, up to 100 stringers had been built, cut up and analysed.

Producing multiple test samples of parts was also useful in verifying the manufacturing procedures and processes. Bartelson observed: "Even if [a part] is perfect it's not production worthy until we prove we can do it more than once."

Building such maturity matters because everything in the CWC is point designed. Bartelson said: "The processes are new and specific to us. All the tooling and equipment is designed to build these specific parts. There's not another one in the world like it. Everything is unique."

With the test samples confirming this maturity, the CWC started work on the first production parts in mid-2017. The first spars and complete panels with co-bonded stringers for the static test airframe were built in the summer, with the first parts for the initial flight test aircraft entering the production process in September 2017.

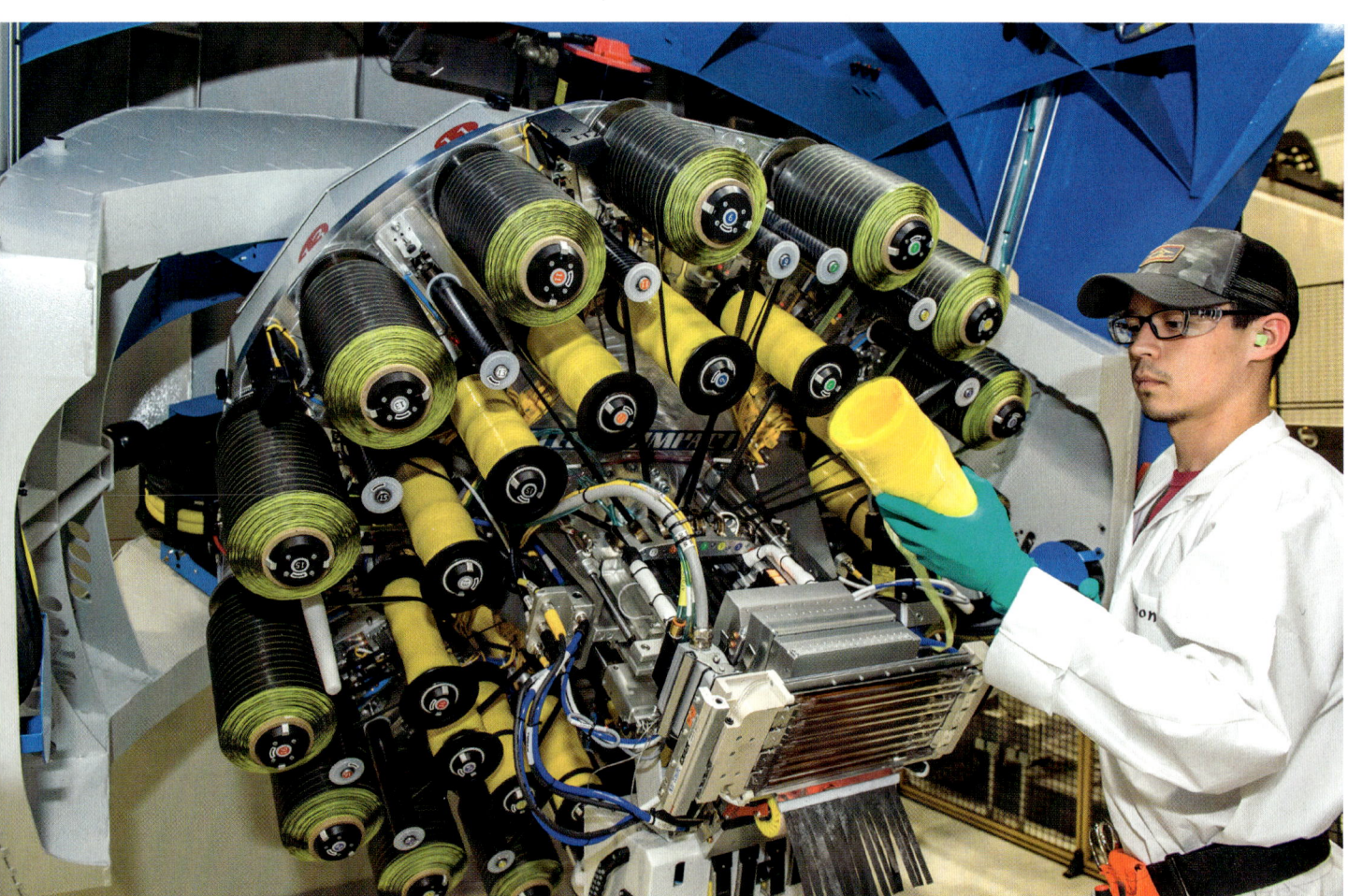

BELOW • *A Boeing employee removes empty spools of carbon fibre material from an automated fibre placement machine used to lay carbon fibre for 777X wing spars.*
BOEING

THE DESTINATION FOR AVIATION ENTHUSIASTS

Visit us today and discover all our latest releases

Image Credit: H Goussé/Airbus

FREE P&P* when you order from our online shop...
shop.keypublishing.com/specials
Call +44 (0)1780 480404 *(Monday to Friday 9am - 5.30pm GMT)*

*Free 2nd class P&P on all UK & BFPO orders. Overseas charges apply.

CABIN

FAR LEFT TOP • *An unusual lighting display projected on to the cabin ceiling of a 777X.* BOEING

FAR LEFT BOTTOM • *Stylish galley areas on board the 777X with a night sky projected on the cabin ceiling generated by the aircraft's lighting system.* BOEING

LEFT • *Larger windows allow more natural light into the 777X's cabin.* BOEING

The Cabin

Mark Broadbent discusses the cabin experience that awaits passengers on board the Boeing 777X.

Passengers will notice differences in the cabin of the 777-9 and 777-8 compared to earlier Triple Sevens. However, in this area, the Dreamliner has again left its mark on the new aircraft.

Discussing the layout Terry Beezhold, 777X vice-president and chief project engineer said: "When we set out to develop the 787 there was a lot of focus on the cabin experience and how we bring the joy back into flying. All the things that were introduced on the 787, the lower cabin altitude, the larger windows, the air purification, the ride quality, work together to provide a much better experience."

The result is the 777Xs will also have a larger window to let more natural light into the cabin (Beezhold said: "We shifted the window belt upwards so everybody whether you're at the window or at the aisle, has a better view.") and LED lighting to create a brighter, lighter atmosphere.

The cabin altitude will also be at what Beezhold called similar levels to the 787's. Boeing has yet to confirm that altitude publicly, but on the Dreamliner the cabin altitude is 6,000ft.

Boeing explains the 787's lower altitude was achieved by a higher level of pressurisation, which the manufacturer stresses was made possible because the composites in the fuselage offer better fatigue resistance.

As noted earlier, however, the 777Xs' fuselages will not be composite, so how is the 787-style cabin altitude possible? Beezhold said although the 777X has an aluminium fuselage: "We understand the margins. We were able to introduce the lower cabin altitude with some minor changes to the airframe. We were able to increase the cabin humidity levels."

ABOVE • *Business class on board a 777X features a staggered seat arrangement.* BOEING

RIGHT • *First class 777X seat arrangement.* BOEING

ENGINE

World's Largest Turbofan Engine

Chris Kjelgaard provides a detailed technological description of the GE9X engine powering the Boeing 777X family.

ABOVE • *The GE9X, which with a 134in fan diameter has the largest fan diameter developed to date for any jet engine.*
GE AVIATION

When GE Aviation's new GE9X large-turbofan engine enters commercial service on the first Boeing 777-9 delivered to a customer, an event now expected to happen in 2025, it will be the largest turbofan powerplant ever to go into service.

Although as a 100,000lb-class-thrust engine the GE9X by design won't offer quite as much maximum take-off thrust as the GE90-115B and GE90-110B1 engines (which respectively power today's 777-300ER and 777-200LR/777F airframes and are the most powerful turbofan engines in the world), it will have a fan diameter six inches greater than that of those engines. In addition to its 134in fan diameter – the largest developed for any jet engine to date – the GE9X will have a corresponding fan-case diameter that also will be bigger than the 154.6in-wide fan case of the two huge GE90 powerplants. Like its siblings, the GE9X will have an overall diameter greater than the fuselage diameter of the Boeing 737 family.

According to Ted Ingling, GE9X programme manager, the reason the GE9X won't offer quite as much maximum take-off thrust as the 115,540lb certificated for the GE90-115B and the 110,760lb certificated for the GE90-110B1 is that it won't need to. He told the author: "That's a testament to Boeing's [777X design] and primarily the wing; they've done a marvellous job in getting the lift drag on the aircraft such that the engine thrust required to fly the bigger 9X-powered aircraft doesn't have to be as high as for the -115B-powered 777-300ER plane."

However, because it has a bigger fan and a larger-diameter fan case than the GE90-115B, the GE9X will be a little heavier - at approximately 20,000lb - than the earlier engine, which weighs 19,316lb dry. That's not to say that the GE9X won't be as fuel efficient. In fact, GE's major design criterion for the 777X engine was to make it 10% more fuel efficient than the predecessor 777-300ER powerplant, and for it to offer 5% lower specific fuel consumption (SFC) than any other engine in or about to enter service on any twin-aisle aircraft.

GE9X Fan Module

GE Aviation expects to achieve that goal using a variety of new technologies, prime among them the improved capabilities that latest-generation computerised aerodynamics modelling offers for airflow design. In the GE9X, this, along with GE Aviation's deep experience of using carbon-

> When GE Aviation's new GE9X large-turbofan engine enters commercial service on the first Boeing 777-9 delivered to a customer, an event now expected to happen in 2025, it will be the largest turbofan powerplant ever to go into service.

fibre composite materials to make three-dimensional airfoils, has resulted in the company being able to construct the engine's massive fan using just 16 fan blades, compared with 22 in the GE90-115B and 18 in the GEnx engine powering the Boeing 787 and 747-8, the GE9X's direct forebear in design terms.

Ingling said: "The ability to use the solidity and aero shaping of the airfoils allowed us to get greater efficiency, thrust flow at speed and reduce the airfoil count. The airfoil count is a big deal for rotating parts, because on the fan blades we can grow the fan diameter to get airflow – bypass ratio is a big play for SFC and noise – but we can also pull the inner radius of the [fan air] flowpath inward, because on the disc that holds on to those blades the radius that encompasses the blade dovetails can come inward, because there are fewer [blade-seating] slots and fewer blades. So, we get a little bit of free real estate by reducing airfoil count relative to getting a bigger flowpath, and of course they are lighter and fewer to maintain." The 16 huge blades allow the GE9X's fan to ingest and propel 3,850lb of air every second at maximum take-off power.

While each of the GE9X's 16 highly 3D curved fan blades is made using, Ingling said, "the same [carbon-fibre] laminate lay-up technology we used on the original GE90, the -115 and the GEnx," another important innovation GE Aviation is introducing is to line each fan blade's leading edge with steel, rather than titanium used to line GE90 and GEnx fan blades. Ingling said: "One of the things you like on a [blade] airfoil is nice thin leading edges, and because steel has got the strength capability over titanium, we were able to thin that leading edge to get even more performance. That goes into the aerodynamics to get higher efficiency and reduced airfoil count."

LEFT • *A computer generated image showing the GE9X's 16 giant fan blades rotating.*
GE AVIATION

BELOW • *The first GE9X engine unit at an early stage of its assembly.*
GE AVIATION

However, at some locations elsewhere in the GE9X fan module GE has replaced metal with polymer matrix composite (PMC) material made of carbon-fibre composite. In addition to making the GE9X's blade platforms – the spacers that sit between the fan blades – and its entire fan case from PMCs, for the first time GE has used PMC material to make the fan module's structural outlet guide vanes (OGVs).

In the fan module, the OGVs connect the outer fan case's aft ring to the inner fan hub as structural elements. They also fulfil another role. The OGVs are designed to straighten out the turbulent airflow propelled behind the fan by the blades before the flow enters the fan duct and then enters the low-pressure compressor booster, for the 10% of the air that flows axially into the engine's core, because the GE9X is designed to produce a 9:1 bypass ratio to make it really quiet in operation.

Ingling said: "That's the first time we have combined those two functions in a composite structure. We've had composite OGVs, but historically had [metal] structural struts or structural OGVs that go between those to carry that load. This is the first vehicle that expands the use of PMCs to fill in both of those elements."

Booster And HPC

The GE9X's three titanium-constructed booster stages are conventional in design. As with the GE90 and GEnx, GE has chosen to install dual-purpose variable bleed valves (VBVs) between the engine's booster and high-pressure compressor (HPC) modules. In the earlier engines the VBVs, which open inward into the core airstream and bleed air from it into the bypass duct, serve to take the airflow load off the HPC, allowing the engine to spool up very quickly when needed, and to extract dust, sand and other debris particles from the core air.

Ingling said: "This engine has a very similar philosophy in using that geometry to extract dust and debris from the engine and it's functional when the [VBV] doors are open, which is generally on the ground or very near the ground. It's proven to be very effective in extracting particles that can be centrifuged, which are the ones that can erode compressor airfoils... keeping the hard stuff out of the engine is

ENGINE

Icing tests were conducted using the first GE9X engine to test.
GE AVIATION

a big deal because that's the stuff you can't recover. When you erode the [compressor] airfoils, the only way to fix that is to disassemble and repair."

While the GE9X's booster is of conventional design and construction, its 11-stage HPC is the most advanced ever designed by GE for a commercial aero engine. Each of the HPC's first five rotating stages is a single-piece blisk, reducing parts count greatly. The six subsequent HPC stages all use hundreds of individual blades, but as it travels through the HPC from front to back the advanced blade airfoils compress the core air by a factor of 27 before it enters the combustor. The blades on the hindmost HPC stage are only about one inch high.

This 27:1 compression ratio gives the GE9X an overall pressure ratio (OPR, the ratio of the pressure of the air entering the combustor compared with the air entering the fan inlet) of 60:1, the highest OPR GE has ever achieved for a commercial engine and probably the highest of any commercial engine in or nearing service. The GE90-115B has an OPR of approximately 40:1 and the GEnx an OPR of about 50:1.

Because air heats up when it is compressed, the air flowing through the HPC's rearmost stages is very hot. GE has constructed the very back GE9X HPC stages from powdered-metal nickel superalloy that Ingling said "we've been using in the turbines for years".

Because the air entering the GE9X combustor is so, the engine's third-generation twin-annular, pre-swirled, mixing (TAPS) combustor is, Ingling said: "running a little hotter than the GEnx", its direct forebear.

Additively Manufactured Parts

Each of the 28 fuel nozzles in the engine's combustor – for comparison, the CFM LEAP-1A engine has 19 fuel nozzles – is additively manufactured, allowing GE to combine what would have been about 28 separate parts in a traditionally manufactured fuel nozzle into just one. In this regard, additive manufacturing is, Ingling said: "a fantastic rapid-prototyping tool and a part-simplification, weight and efficiency mechanism to simplify the engine and get better performance out of it".

Although as a very large engine the GE9X is not an ideal vehicle for employing additively manufactured parts, because, according to Ingling, most of the readily available additive-manufacturing machines are small

The GE9X's three titanium-constructed booster stages are conventional in design. As with the GE90 and GEnx, GE has chosen to install dual-purpose variable bleed valves (VBVs) between the engine's booster and high-pressure compressor (HPC) modules.

ENGINE

and make small parts, the big turbofan does make use of other additively manufactured parts in addition to its fuel nozzles. Its heat exchanger, swirler, particle separator and T25 sensors (engine-control temperature sensors located in the mid-stage between the booster and HPC modules) are all additively manufactured, as are the titanium-aluminide (TiAl) blades for an unspecified number of the stages in the back end of the GE9X's six-stage, all-TiAl low-pressure turbine (LPT) module.

Ingling said the GE9X's TAPS III combustor provides: "a very homogenous, highly mixed air/fuel system that gives us lean burning [and] gets rid of hot streaks", unlike combustors using rich-burn-quench ignition cycles that burn hot and try to homogenise the exhaust gas to a uniform temperature by the time it gets to the high-pressure turbine (HPT) first-stage nozzle. But: "This has so much swirl in it that it mixes the fuel very finely. When [the air/fuel mixture] burns it's a much more uniform temperature profile both radially across the top of the passage and between cups, fuel nozzle to fuel nozzle. So, you have HPT nozzles that statically sit behind the fuel nozzles and having a uniform [temperature] profile into those makes for a more durable and predictable design for those nozzles."

CMCs and Air Cooling

A particularly important technological advance in the GE9X is that, building on the pioneering use of ceramic matrix composite (CMC) materials in making the first-stage HPT nozzle shroud for the CFM International LEAP engine (GE Aviation is a 50% partner in CFM), the bigger engine has five categories of CMC parts. This represents the widest use of CMCs in any commercial engine to date.

Ingling said: "The GE9X expands the journey to other static components: two nozzles, two liners and the shroud."

THIS IMAGE • *The GE9X second engine to test at GE Aviation's Peebles, Ohio facility in May 2017.* GE AVIATION

RIGHT • *Five parts in the GE9X are manufactured from ceramic matrix composites (two nozzles, two liners and the shroud) which were demonstrated using a GEnx demonstrator engine.* GE AVIATION

BELOW • *GE Aviation's Boeing 747 Flying Test Bed fitted with a GE9X engine mounted on the inner left pylon. Unique to the GE9X, the pylon cantilevers the engine out in front of the wing's leading edge at a 7° upward tilt.* GE AVIATION

The combustor's inner and outer lining is made of CMC material, as are the engine's first-stage and second-stage HPT nozzles and its first-stage HPT shroud. He continued: "Three things came together for the LEAP programme: it had a value proposition that made sense for the engine, the ability to manufacture it in volume, and the capability and technology of it was validated. Those three elements created the right environment to introduce it. With that proof, and the GE9X overlapping it, we took it to the next level while keeping it to the static structure... In the timeframe for the GE9X, the convergence of the ability to design, manufacture and produce and a value proposition kept it to five parts."

The GE9X employs the technique used in most modern turbofan engines of diverting bypass or compressor air to manage the temperatures of the HPT and LPT casings, thus shrinking or expanding the metal casings to provide active clearance control that minimises the distances between the casing linings and the tips of the blade airfoils rotating inside them. This minimises airflow loss due to turbulent air seeping over the tips of the blades and maximises the blades' aerodynamic efficiency, improving the overall efficiency of the engine.

In addition, however, the GE9X makes use of two new blade-cooling technologies, one first introduced in the CFM LEAP engine and one new to the GE9X itself. As in the LEAP engine, GE designed the software for the GE9X's full authority digital engine control computer so the computer can vary the amounts of HPC bleed air that are sent to the first HPT stage's inducer and blade cooling-air circuits during different phases of flight.

During low-thrust, low-temperature phases of operation, such as cruise, engine idle and perhaps aircraft taxiing, the HPT first-stage blades (made of a powdered nickel superalloy) require much less cooling than during high-temperature, high-thrust phases of flight such as take-off and approach. This modulation allows the engine to bleed off only as much HPT cooling air as is absolutely required at any time of the flight, increasing the amount of core airflow, and improving the engine's overall performance.

The second new blade-cooling technology used in the GE9X, for the first time in any commercial engine, is a new HPT blade-manufacturing technique that GE has industrialised at its castings and forging plant in Ohio. Ingling said: "[This] gives the flexibility to the heat-transfer and mechanical-design teams to create cooling circuitry that is not able to be produced by conventional methods. It's a way to get more efficient cooling for the inside of the airfoil to enable a more uniform, durable blade while getting some performance out of it without sacrificing anything. It's a flexibility that is enabled by this manufacturing process that allows the blade designers more freedom, like additive [manufacturing] gives more freedom to designers to come up with lighter-weight structures, a similar philosophy."

777X Milestones

Mark Ayton and Mark Broadbent etch out the 777X's big milestones to date.

Singapore Airlines Buys In

On October 23, 2017, the White House was used as the venue for a ceremony during which Boeing and Singapore Airlines announced a multi-billion-dollar deal for 20 777-9s and 19 787-10s. The event took place in the presence of President Trump and Prime Minister of Singapore Lee Hsien Loong.

Boeing had previously attributed the $13.8 billion order to an unidentified customer. As of May 2024, Singapore Airlines has orders for a further 11 777-9 aircraft.

Singapore Airlines' CEO Goh Choon Phong said: "SIA has been a Boeing customer for many decades and we are pleased to have finalised this major order for widebody aircraft, which will enable us to continue operating a modern and fuel-efficient fleet. These new aircraft will also provide the SIA Group with new growth opportunities, allowing us to expand our network and offer even more travel options for our customers."

First Centre Wing Section

Subaru Corporation announced on February 9, 2018 that its aerospace company had completed production of the first 777X centre wing section and its integration with the main landing gear wheel wells. Production of the first Boeing 777X centre wing work package took place at the Handa Plant in Aichi Prefecture, Subaru's manufacturing facility for Boeing 777 and Boeing 787 centre wing boxes.

Subaru has participated in the 777X programme since the initial design development phase, and is now responsible for the side-of-body section, the centre wing box, integration of the centre wing section with the main landing gear wheel wells, main landing gear doors, and the forward wing-to-body fairings.

Production Kicks Off

Three months after Subaru's centre wing section announcement, Boeing released photos showing the forward fuselage section of the first 777-9 airframe at its Everett assembly plant. Wings for this airframe and the first

ABOVE • *Aircraft WH002, the second flight test aircraft made its first flight from Everett-Paine Field on April 30, 2020.*
BOEING

> Sales of the 777X have remained relatively slow since the aircraft's launch over a decade ago, with well under 500 orders having been placed by May 2024.

flight test aircraft (WH001), the second 777-9 to be assembled, were also in production; fuselage assembly of WH001 started in late 2018.

At the time of the 777-9 production announcement, updated provisional Airplane Characteristics for Airport Planning for the 777-9 and 777-8 variants, provided details about the functionality of the folding wing tip (FWT) mechanism designed for the 777X.

According to the document, during taxi for departure, the 777X will have the FWT folded. Once a predetermined location on the airport has been passed, a position that ensures clearance from ground objects, the flight crew will manually initiate the command for the FWT to extend and lock into position. This procedure will be completed prior to the aircraft arriving at the runway hold-short line. The document reads: "Due to the unique geometry of each airport, it will not be practical to automate the extension of the FWT and the extension action will be left to the flight deck crew for manual operation when required." On landing, the FWT control logic will automatically fold the wingtip after the aircraft has touched down and ground speed is below 50kt, which will take 20 seconds in normal conditions.

In the event of abnormal conditions, the crew will be alerted by a message generated by the engine indicating and crew alerting system, and a non-normal FWT operation plan will be invoked. For example, in the event of a high-speed rejected take-off, the FWT will automatically fold if the aircraft

777X MILESTONES

achieves a rejected take-off ground speed of 85kt or above, with the wingtip folding once the aircraft has decelerated below 50kt ground speed. The 85kt threshold is the same threshold for activating RTO autobrakes and speed brakes.

Roll Out

In early September 2018, one year after assembly started on the first Boeing 777X airframe, the aircraft was rolled out. The airframe involved was the first static test aircraft which was used for structural strength testing and did not feature a nose cone, horizontal stabiliser, vertical tail plane or avionics systems, but it was equipped with the folding wingtip (FWT) mechanism.

Power-On

At the time of the static test jet roll-out, the first flight test aircraft WH001, later registered N779XW (c/n 64240) was in final assembly. In early December

ABOVE • *Singapore Airlines joined the 777X club on October 23, 2017, when it announced a multi-billion-dollar deal for 20 777-9s - since increased to 31.* BOEING

LEFT • *Long-time Boeing 777 operator British Airways has signed an agreement for up to 18 777-9s.* BOEING

2018, Boeing powered on WH001. The milestone followed the final body join of the nose, mid and aft fuselage sections in November. Fuselage join was another major 777X production milestone. At the time, Josh Binder, vice president and general manager of the 777X, said Boeing was hitting its milestones as expected in developing the 777X.

When WH001 was rolled-out from the Everett final assembly line on March 13, 2019, Boeing held a closed event, not open to the media. That very day, Boeing Commercial Airplanes was making the headlines around the world for the worst of reasons: the second crash involving a Boeing 737 MAX. The aircraft, ET-AVJ, operated by Ethiopian Airlines on a flight from Addis Ababa to Nairobi, Kenya crashed six minutes after take-off killing all 157 people on board. The same day that the Federal Aviation Administration grounded the type. One hundred and thirty-five days earlier, a 737 MAX 8 operated by Lion Air on a flight from Jakarta to Pangkai Pinang, Indonesia crashed into the sea a few minutes after take-off killing all 189 people on board.

British Airways orders 777X

In April 2019, British Airways announced it had chosen the Boeing 777X to re-equip part of its long-haul fleet, signing an agreement with the manufacturer for up to 42 777-9s, comprising 18 orders and 24 options. Prior to the outbreak of the COVID-19 pandemic and the subsequent widely reported production and certification delays at Boeing, the jets were due to be delivered between 2022 and 2025, now clearly delayed still further.

British Airways will use its 777-9s to serve the carrier's long-haul trunk routes, as per its 18 Airbus A350-1000s.

Willie Walsh, the chief executive officer of British Airways' parent company IAG, described the 777-9 as a "perfect replacement to the 747-400", saying: "This aircraft will provide further cost efficiencies and environmental benefits with fuel cost per seat improvements of 30% compared to the 747. It also provides an enhanced passenger experience."

Ordering the 777-9 continues British Airways' long relationship with the Triple Seven, the carrier was a launch customer for the original 777-200 back in 1990, the initial European operator in 1995 and remains one of the largest 777 operators worldwide. Operating 777-9s means the airline will gain from the commonality in spares and maintenance with the current 777 and shared type ratings for crews. This order was placed in a pre-COVID world, and it remains to be seen how the pandemic and further delays will alter British Airways' long-haul fleet plan given the slump in demand. The 24 options have not so far been taken up.

Sales of the 777X have remained relatively slow since the aircraft's launch over a decade ago with fewer than 500 orders placed by May, 2024.

First Flight Delay

The first flight of the Boeing 777X was pushed out to early 2020 due to development issues with the aircraft's General Electric GE9X turbofan engines, Boeing disclosed in its Q2 2019 financial results.

In a statement the company said: "The 777X programme is progressing well through pre-flight testing. While the company is still targeting late 2020 for the first delivery of the 777X, there is a significant risk to this schedule given engine challenges, which are delaying the first flight until early 2020."

More specifically, the problem presenting the challenges to Boeing was with the stator vane in the second stage of the GE9X's high-pressure compressor. In the compressor, energy is added to the gas by the rotor blades, then converted to static pressure by the stator vanes (stationary airfoils).

The problem was discovered during early reliability testing of a GE9X engine fitted to WH001 (the first flight test aircraft) in late May 2019. This forced a redesign that pushed back engine certification into the autumn and, in turn, the expected first flight date into early 2020.

Boeing rolled out WH001 (registered N779XW, c/n 64240) at Everett in March 2019 and originally planned to fly the aircraft in June.

Despite the delay, Boeing initially insisted it was planning for the 777-9 to achieve type certification and entry into service by the end of 2020. That was an ambitious timescale, and at the very least would have involved an aggressive flight testing schedule.

Asked what processes had to take place to gain certification of the GE9X last year that enabled the first certified engines to be delivered to Everett in October 2019, Boeing replied: "To help ensure the safety and performance of new aircraft, we thoroughly test systems in ground tests before first flight. The engines are part of that overall ground test programme. GE had been running the GE9X engines through some rigorous conditions that went beyond what would normally be encountered in operation on wing, 'fatigue' type tests meant to prove the engine's endurance and reliability. During some of these tests, GE detected a durability issue in a component in the high pressure compressor. GE enhanced the component's design

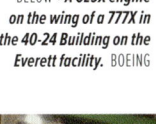

BELOW • *A GE9X engine on the wing of a 777X in the 40-24 Building on the Everett facility.* BOEING

> Boeing conducted a successful first flight of the second 777X flight test aircraft on April 30, 2020. Captain Ted Grady, 777X project pilot, and Captain Van Chaney, 777/777X chief pilot, flew for two hours and 58 minutes over Washington state before landing at Boeing Field, King County International Airport, Seattle at 2:02pm local time.

777X MILESTONES

and retrofitted test engines to reflect the new design. We worked closely with GE through the process. As with any development programme, we are thoughtful and deliberate, taking the time to get the details right with safety as our top priority."

Aircraft WH001 finally took off from Everett-Paine Field on the type's maiden flight at 10:09 local time on January 25, 2020, landing at Boeing Field, King County International Airport in Seattle after 3 hours and 52 minutes.

Depressurization Failure

In September 2019, Boeing was thrown another curve ball. During stress testing, the 777X static test aircraft (the first airframe to be built) suffered an explosive depressurisation during final load stage. According to the Seattle Times, damage to the aircraft included a rupture in the fuselage skin just behind the wing, and the blow out of a passenger door.

Asked what the consequences of the failure were to the 777X programme, Boeing said: "In the final load testing of the static test aircraft, our team conducted a test that involves bending the wings of the aircraft up to a level far beyond anything expected in commercial service. A testing issue occurred during the final minutes of the test, at approximately 99 percent of the final test loads, and involved a depressurization of the aft fuselage. The test team followed all safety protocols. This will not have a significant impact on the design, and we do not see any impact from the test on the overall programme schedule. We remain fully focused on safety as our highest priority as we subject the 777X to a rigorous test programme."

WH002 Completes First Flight

Boeing conducted a successful first flight of the second 777X flight test aircraft on April 30, 2020. Captain Ted Grady, 777X project pilot, and Captain Van Chaney, 777/777X chief pilot, flew for two hours and 58 minutes over Washington state before landing at Boeing Field, King County International Airport, Seattle at 2:02pm local time.

Designated WH002, N779XX (c/n 64241) is the second of four such aircraft and is being used to test handling characteristics and other performance aspects. An array of equipment, sensors and monitoring devices installed throughout the cabin allows the on board team to document and evaluate the aircraft's response to test conditions in real time.

ABOVE • *Aircraft WH001 in the final assembly position in the 40-24 Building.* BOEING

RIGHT • BOEING

> Willie Walsh, the chief executive officer of British Airways' parent company IAG, described the 777-9 as a "perfect replacement to the 747-400", saying: "This aircraft will provide further cost efficiencies and environmental benefits with fuel cost per seat improvements of 30% compared to the 747.

Boeing's 777X test plan lays out a comprehensive series of test events and conditions on the ground and in the air to demonstrate the safety and reliability of the design.

To date, crews have flown the first aircraft WH001 at a variety of flap settings, speeds, altitudes, and system settings as part of the initial evaluation of the flight envelope. With initial airworthiness demonstrated, test pilots are now flying with a test director, flight engineers and mechanics, instrumentation engineers, and flight-test engineers who monitor testing instead of relying solely on a ground-based telemetry station, unlocking testing at greater distances.

Cautious Change

Discussing the 777X during the Q2 2020 earnings call on July 29, Boeing president, chief executive officer and director David Calhoun said: "We continue to execute the flight testing phase of our rigorous test programme. As we look toward entry into service, we have adjusted the timing of the first 777-9 delivery to 2022 versus our prior forecast of 2021. This reflects our assessment of the development

and test timeline, feedback from our customers, and projected impacts from COVID-19. We are also incorporating lessons learned from the 737 certification process. We will continue to manage the risks inherent in any development programme. We continue to expect to deliver 777s at an average rate of approximately 2.5 per month in 2020. We will take a measured approach to the 777X rate ramp as we look to minimize the amount of change incorporation work by managing the number of aircraft produced prior to entry into service.

Due to market uncertainties, driven primarily by the impacts of COVID-19 and moving the 777X certification and delivery to 2022, we now plan to reduce the combined 777/777X production rate to two per month in 2021 versus our previous plan of three per month in 2021."

More Maiden Flights

Boeing's third Boeing 777-9 flight test aircraft WH003 registered N779XY (c/n 64242) painted in Boeing's light livery took off from Everett-Paine Field at 13:55 local time. The aircraft flew two approaches at Moses Lake Airport in eastern Washington state before landing at Boeing Field, King County International Airport in Seattle at the end of a two hour 45-minute flight on August 3.

WH003's maiden flight was welcome news from the 777X programme coming just five days after David Calhoun had announced the customer delivery delay.

Boeing specified the avionics system, auxiliary power unit, flight loads and propulsion performance as some of the test events to be undertaken by WH003, adding that it is pleased with the progress made to date with the 777X flight test programme.

Just 49 days later on September 21, Boeing's fourth flight test 777-9, N779XZ (c/n 64243), made its maiden flight.

Taking off from Everett-Paine Field, flying to Moses Lake for some approaches before recovering to Boeing Field, King County International Airport in Seattle, WH004 completed a safe, successful first flight. Boeing specified cabin systems and extended operations as two test programmes to be undertaken by WH004.

Delivery Delays

In April 2022, Boeing again delayed 777X deliveries due to production and certification issues. In November of that same year, it emerged that a GE9X engine on one of the test aircraft had suffered technical faults a month earlier, leading to another pause for further investigations. As of May 2024, no deliveries are expected by customers before late 2025, and some expect that date to be pushed back into 2026 at the earliest.

777X PROGRAMME LATEST

Latest on the
777X

With the co-operation of Boeing Commercial Airplanes in Seattle, **Mark Ayton** provides the latest details about the 777X programme.

Boeing, like all aircraft manufacturers, makes exciting performance claims about its aircraft. The 777X is no exception. To clearly understand the claims made, the company kindly responded to a series of questions.

Boeing says the 777X is the most efficient twin-engine jet, unmatched in every aspect of performance. Clarifying which types of airliners the 777X is compared to and which aspects of performance the company refers to, Boeing said: "The Boeing 777-8 and 777-9, along with the 787 Dreamliner, advance the world's most efficient twin-aisle family. The 777-8 offers more versatility than the competition, the Airbus A350-1000. The 777-9 is in a market space all its own, with no direct competitor. Performance is measured in respect to payload range and fuel efficiency. The 777X family of airplanes can fly farther with more payload than the competition or today's 777. Fuel consumption per seat, a common measurement in the industry, is the lowest ever for this class of airplane."

The company says the 777X features new breakthroughs in aerodynamics. What are they? In its response, Boeing said: "The all-new, composite, 235ft 5in span wing is key to the unrivalled performance advantage of the 777X. Freed from traditional infrastructure-driven constraints, the 777X wing has 22ft 11in more span than that of the A350-1000, resulting in 5% better lift/drag. It's simple and reliable folding wingtip design enables high-span efficiency while maintaining taxiway and gate compatibility with today's 777. In addition to the all-new composite wing, the 777X features variable camber wing technology, blended-raked wingtips, a new tail, and laminar flow engine nacelles. The 777X also incorporates the latest 3D airfoil design due to improved computational fluid dynamics. In total, the 777X will have the most advanced aerodynamic technology of any airliner."

www.key.aero 109

777X PROGRAMME LATEST

Similarly, Boeing says new breakthroughs are featured in the type's GE9X engines. What are those design breakthroughs in the GE9X engine? Boeing reckons the GE9X on the 777X is a fully optimized design (including core and fan size) that takes advantage of the latest technologies, once again resulting in a step change in fuel efficiency. Boeing said: "The GE9X will also benefit from unique GE technologies such as fourth-generation composite fan blades, ceramic matrix composite components and advanced engine aerodynamics. These exclusive GE technologies contribute to an overall pressure ratio significantly higher than any existing large turbofan."

Driven by the need to produce aircraft that burn less fuel and produce less emissions, Boeing says the 777X will deliver 10% lower, so which parameters is this based on, and what types of jets is performance compared to? Boeing said: "The 777-9 is 10% more fuel efficient per seat than the competition [the A350-1000]. The lower fuel consumption is a result of 5% better aerodynamics and the latest engine technology with the lowest SFC [specific fuel consumption] in its class. The new efficient core has the highest pressure ratio due to an unconstrained design enabling a generational improvement in fuel use and emissions."

Operating costs are of primary importance to an operator. In recognition of this requirement Boeing says the 777X offers 10% lower operating costs than the competition, so which parameters is this claim based on, and how is this claim justified? In response, Boeing affirmed the 777-9 offers 10% lower relative cash operating cost per seat than the competition. It said: "Operating cost is compared at a 6,000nm trip and two-class seating. Components of operational cost include fuel, total maintenance, flight crew, airport, navigational and landing fees. For both fuel consumption and economic costs, Boeing uses a set of standard mission rules that are applied to all aircraft comparisons. Competitive aircraft performance is evaluated based on public industry data such as size, weight and engine characteristics."

Away from the 777X's environmental and economic credentials, Boeing says the aircraft offers low-risk, profitable growth, and industry-leading reliability. The author was interested to know what data was used to make these determinations and how Boeing justifies each one? The company gave an individual response to each.

Low risk: With 10% lower fuel consumption and operating economics than the competitor's best, the 777X can serve any market at lower costs than today's aircraft. This generational improvement in efficiency allows airlines to try new markets or increase frequency to existing ones while generating more revenue through additional seats and available cargo.

Profitable growth: The 777X is perfectly positioned for the future commercial air travel market. Compared to the very popular 777-300ER, the 777X offers customers the choice to either reach farther destinations and open new city pairs with the 777-8 or grow an existing market with additional capacity of the 777-9. In addition, the inherent benefits of an efficient, unconstrained wing design enable the 777X family to serve a multitude of networks such as long, ultra-long, high and hot, and high-payload missions.

Industry-leading reliability: The 777X builds upon the world's most reliable twin-aisle, the 777-300ER. Consistently featuring a 99.5% dispatch reliability is truly remarkable and speaks to the superior design of the aircraft and our focus on continuing to improve fleet reliability. The 777X utilises the proven, reliable systems of the 777-300ER

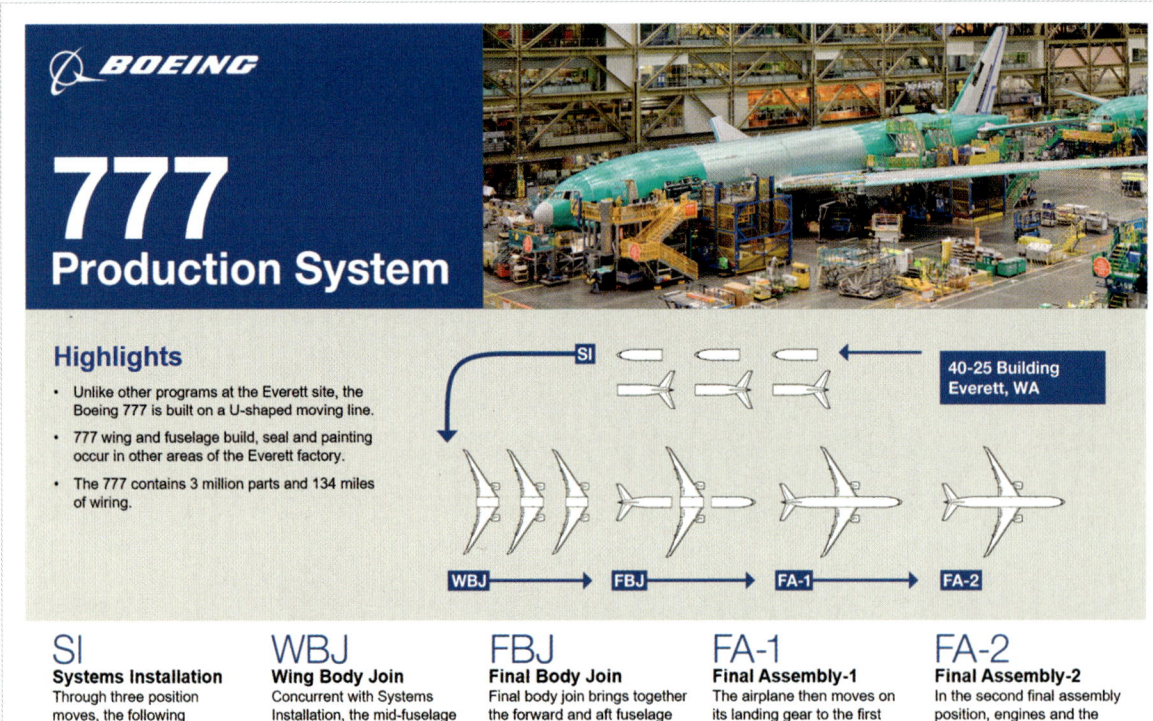

Figure 1

A diagram showing the main production build sequence of the 777 production system housed in the 40-25 Building at Everett. BOEING

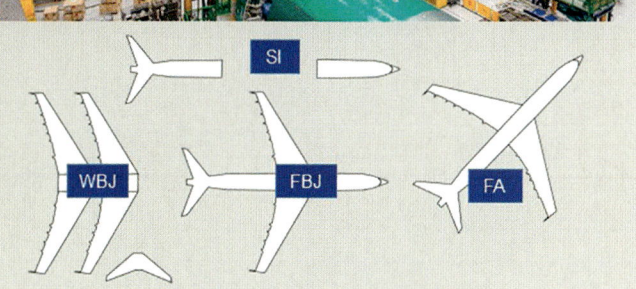

Figure 2

A diagram showing the low-rate initial production system where the first several 777X aircraft were built. BOEING

777X Low-Rate Initial Production System

Highlights
- To avoid disruption on the 777 line in the 40-25 building, the first several 777X airplanes were built in the low-rate initial production line in the 40-24 building.
- The 777X wing and fuselage build, seal and painting occurred in other areas of the Everett site.
- Today, 777-9 airplanes are built within the 40-25 building on the 777 line.
- The 777X flight test program began in 2020, and Boeing continues to work toward delivery in 2025.

SI — Systems Installation
Through three position moves, the following systems were installed on the forward and aft fuselage sections: wires, insulation blankets and sidewall panels. Systems Installation also is where the flight deck is assembled and the horizontal and vertical stabilizers are attached.

WBJ — Wing Body Join
Concurrent with Systems Installation, the mid-fuselage section was joined with the wings in the wing-body join area.

FBJ — Final Body Join
Final body join brings together the forward and aft fuselage sections with the joined wing-body assembly. This is where the airplane came together for the first time, the landing gear was attached, and the leading and trailing flaps and additional systems were installed.

FA — Final Assembly
The airplane then moved on its landing gear to final assembly for functional testing before leaving the factory.

www.boeing.com/777X

ABOVE • *A computer-generated image of the 777X's composite wing showing its profile and sweep.* BOEING

while introducing more modern components that are connected via an advanced on board network, giving flight and maintenance crews access to real-time system analytics.

Engineering

Externally, Boeing's final design configuration for the 777X may not look all that different to the 300ER. That's not a fair proposition. In reality the 777X features a range of new systems and features, but what has changed in terms of individual components and hardware? In its response, Boeing said: "We follow a disciplined design, development and testing process to optimize our designs so that we deliver maximum value for our customers. Those [customers] with the 777 family, the most successful twin-aisle family of all time, asked that we maintain similar reliability while improving the economics further with the 777X. We leveraged the design of the 777, including the aluminium fuselage, with enhancements to improve manufacturing, performance, or durability such as using more composites and advanced alloys.

These include features and technologies developed for the Dreamliner, as Boeing confirmed: "As the most successful twin-aisle family

777X PROGRAMME LATEST

> "The Boeing 777-8 and 777-9, along with the 787 Dreamliner, advance the world's most efficient twin-aisle family. The 777-8 offers more versatility than the competition, the Airbus A350-1000. The 777-9 is in a market space all its own, with no direct competitor." Boeing

ABOVE • **Lift-off for the 777X's maiden flight on January 25, 2020.** BOEING

RIGHT • **A diagram showing the 777X suppliers of the major structures and propulsion components and systems.** BOEING

ever, the 777 is the unequivocal market leader in long-haul service, delivering proven performance, profitability and reliability and a great passenger experience. We are keenly focused on developing and delivering a superior aircraft that ensures the 777 family remains the market leader. To that end, the 777X leverages proven 787 technologies where they benefit our customers and their passengers. In addition to the composite wing, 787 technologies on the 777X include laminar flow nacelles, flight deck displays, flight controls, other systems enhancements, and cabin experience benefits (for example, Smoother Ride Technology, enhanced cabin altitude and humidity and large windows with available dimming).

"The 777X represents a generational leap in technology with an all-new high-span all-new composite wing and a new high bypass ratio engine: two key anchors that will ensure the 777X remains the most fuel-efficient commercial aircraft in its category.

"We are also introducing innovations that will ensure an exceptional experience, including a new, spacious, cabin architecture that can be customized easily throughout the same aircraft – a true canvas for airlines – and sculpted sidewalls for a wider cabin (4in wider than today's 777; up to 16in wider than the competition) that provides more space in every class and accommodates comfortable 10-abreast economy class seating.

"We use composite materials in our designs where they provide optimal value. On the 777X, most notably that is the world's largest single-piece composite wing skin as well as the empennage and the floor beams (first pioneered on the 777). Furthermore, for years Boeing has used additive manufacturing to produce commercial aircraft parts. Some examples of 777X parts include ducts, stowage pockets and footrests."

Production

Today, Boeing's gargantuan production facility in Everett, Washington is home to the 767 and 777/777X widebody families. Everett is also where Boeing began 777X production, using a transition approach to its final assembly process. The company explained: "Initially we are using the 40-24 building for low-rate production. This allows us to focus on production while we prepare for a smooth transition to the main 777 line, which is in the 40-25 building." Boeing supplied two infographics (Figure 1 and Figure 2) to show the assembly positions of the concurrent production systems in use; one for the initial low-rate 777X line and today's combined line in the 40-25 building.

The final assembly process used at the Everett facility depends on components

supplied by Boeing facilities from around the United States and other companies from around the world. Boeing supplied a third infographic (Figure 3) to show all of the major structure assemblies used on a 777X.

Flight Deck

Boeing was asked to provide further details (to those already outlined in this publication) about the many updates incorporated in the 777X's flight deck systems. In its response, the company stated it would be able to speak more in depth once the 777X is certified and the first aircraft has been delivered to its customer. Boeing said: "Our focus now is the continued development and testing of the aircraft. The 777X flight deck includes the best of both today's 777 and the 787, along with new technologies, to increase efficiency, connectivity and situational awareness."

Boeing noted that several features contribute to additional situational awareness and enhanced safety, including synthetic runway presentation on the head-up display for low-visibility approach and landings, a GPS-based landing system (GLS), integrated approach navigation and new alerts for in-air and on-ground overrun conditions.

Other flight deck features include:
- Head-up displays.
- Large-format displays similar to those on the 787, with new touchscreen technology – a first in commercial air transport. Touchscreen technology adds value for customers and helps streamline operations, plus the interface is more in line with pilot expectations given today's technology (e.g., iPads used for electronic flight bag or EFB, and planning functions off-aircraft). Pilots can also interface directly with the flight management computer format as they do on the 777.
- Improved connectivity with the pilot's portable devices (such as the EFB) and the ability to integrate EFB information onto the forward displays. For example, pilots can display the on board performance tool from the EFB on the forward displays for pre-flight calculations, and for briefings they can place approach charts on the forward displays too.
- Autobrake system to target specific runway exits. Based on flight planning, pilots can define which exit is

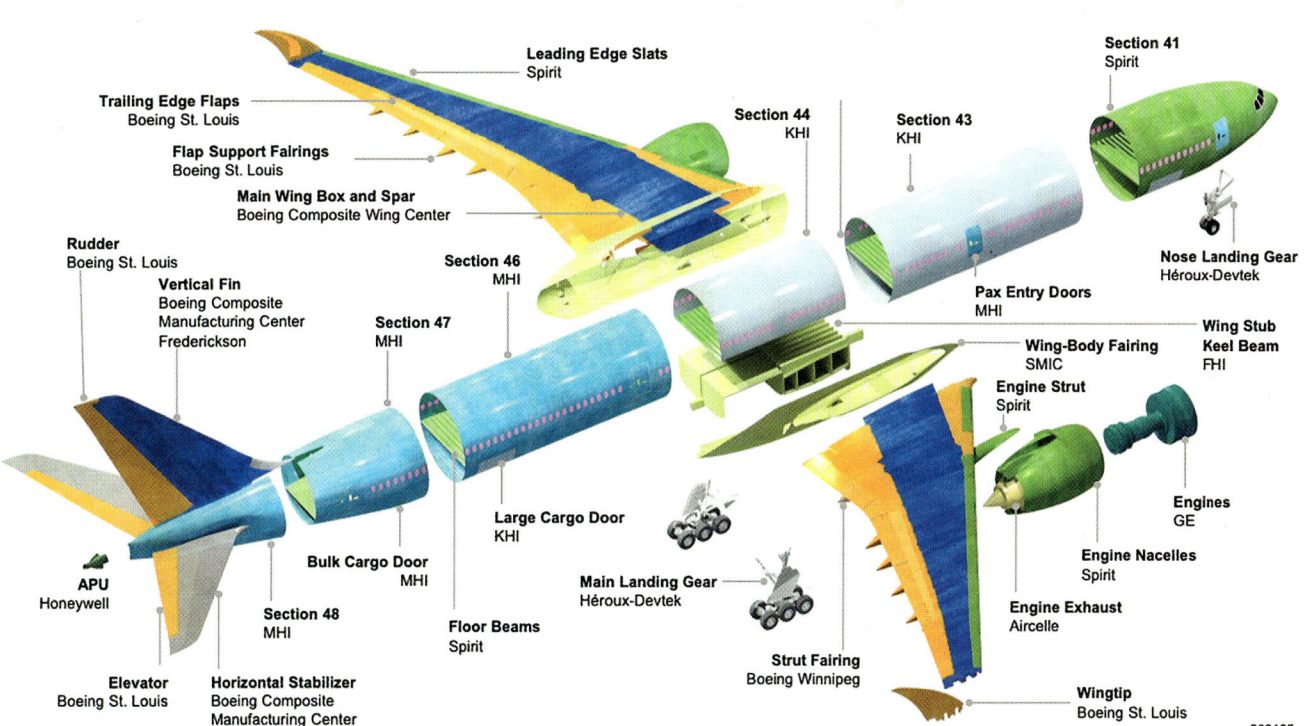

www.key.aero 113

777X PROGRAMME LATEST

> The final assembly process used at Boeing's Everett facility depends on components supplied by Boeing facilities from around the United States and other companies from around the world.

optimal for their gate; on the runway auto-braking will decelerate the aircraft to that exit for more efficient runway occupancy and taxi-in.

- Systems controls that are common to the 777, and overhead panel arrangement consistent with the 777 and the 787.

- Features to enhance pilot comfort, include newly designed seats, a quieter cabin environment, new LED lighting and improved sun shades and visors.

Flight-test

Boeing continues to conduct a comprehensive series of tests and conditions, on the ground and in the air, to demonstrate the safety and reliability of the 777X design. The latest phase of a rigorous year-long flight test programme of the 777-9 began in January 2020. The 777-9 test programme includes the fatigue and static test airframes and four dedicated flight-test aircraft. Table 1 lists the types of testing to be conducted by each of the four 777-9 aircraft.

Other aspects of the flight test programme include aerodynamics, engine performance and fuel flow, airspeed and high-speed testing, followed by more advanced events involving system and engine failures, stall testing to determine if the jet has enhanced stall protection, take-off performance in hot and cold temperatures, and with crosswinds, tailwinds and headwinds. Other more complex tests follow such as, velocity, minimum control ground tests, full-brake rejected take-offs, crosswind landings, endurance, and tests to determine the minimum speed at which the aircraft will fly.

Boeing has taken lessons learned from the 737 MAX programme and applied them to the 777X to ensure its preparations for type certification are in the best possible condition. Boeing is not planning to certify the 777X as a new aircraft but a 777 variant.

Boeing did not provide any information about the ongoing 777X flight test programme but said: "We generally don't provide forward-looking information about our test plans. At a high level, we are fully focused on safety as our highest priority as we continue to subject the 777-9 to a rigorous test program. Flight testing began in January 2020, and today all four of our dedicated flight-test airplanes are flying. Flight testing is proceeding well, and we are pleased with the progress we are making."

BOTTOM • *WH001 flies with its landing gears extended during the first flight on January 25, 2020.* BOEING

Boeing's 777-9 Flight Test Fleet

Test aircraft	Test programmes
WH001 First flight: January 25, 2020	Operating envelope expansion, flight controls, avionics and related systems, brakes, flutter, icing, low-speed aerodynamics, stability, and control
WH002 First flight: April 30, 2020	Auto lands, ground effects, stability, and control
WH003 First flight: August 2, 2020	Auxiliary power unit, avionics, flight loads, engine performance including high-speed nautical air miles (NAMS) fuel consumption tests, and inflight engine starts
WH004 First flight: September 20, 2020	Environmental control system, extended twin-engine operations, functionality, noise, general functionality, and reliability